# LAND
# NAV

BRONSTON CLOUGH

## BASIC TO ADVANCED
### (WLC, ALC, SLC, RANGER, SF & DELTA)

Typesetting and layout by Amber Cornett
Cover design by Matthew Dail

## Land Nav: Basic to Advanced

PUBLISHED BY

# MENTOR®
## ENTERPRISES, INC.

123 Castle Dr. STE C, Madison, AL 35758

info@mentorinc.us

Printed in USA by Mentor Enterprises, Inc.

1st Edition, 2014

ISBN-13: 978-1-940370-02-6
ISBN-10: 1-940370-02-7

The views expressed in this book are those of Bronston Clough and do not reflect the official policy or position of the United States Army, Defense Department, or the United States Government. No copyrights are claimed on material created by the United States Government.

# Dedication

To my wife, Angie who I love more than ever. Thank you for your constant support. You are the epitome of a Proverbs 31 woman! Our boys are lucky to have you as their mama and I'm lucky to have you as my wife. I can't wait to see what God still has in store for us. I love you!

To Weston and Holden, I couldn't be more proud. I light up when I get home from work and see you guys. I know I make mistakes and I'm thankful you all forgive me. I love you both more than you'll ever know. God has big plans for both of you!

# Table of Contents

## Basic

# Advanced

**Updates and corrections can be found online:**
http://asktop.net/land-1ed
Access Code: **LN16CLOU**

# Introduction

In today's world, Soldiers rely heavily on their GPS. What are you going to do if you run out of batteries or the satellites go down? You better know how to use a map and compass. Land Navigation is the skill that sets apart the Army's elite Soldiers from the average Soldiers.

Unfortunately, the Army doesn't do a very good job of teaching land navigation. This book will be your ultimate trainer. Whether you just want to improve your navigation skills for hunting and hiking or you aspire to attend the Army's toughest schools and selection courses, this is the book for you.

The skills in this book range from basic to advanced. The "Basic" section of the book covers the fundamentals and basic skills necessary to be able to navigate. Much of that information is also found in FM's and Soldier's Manuals, which are very few in print these days with everything being digital. The "Advanced" section covers field expedient methods, route planning as well as tips and tricks and a section on the Ranger School Land Nav course and the SFAS Land Nav course.

The contributors to this book were Ranger Instructors, Special Forces, and a 1st SFOD-D officer. They completed many Army land nav courses including the most difficult land nav tests the Army has to offer. I think you'll find their insight helpful and useful. If you apply what is in this book you will be the best Soldier at Land Nav in your unit and won't have any problem with basic and advanced course land nav tests, EIB land nav, or Ranger, SFAS, and Delta Selection. Make your own luck!

# CHAPTER 1:
# BASICS

## MARGINAL INFORMATION

**STOP!!!!** Do NOT skip this section. Understanding the marginal information on a map is critical to being able to use the map. What is marginal information? It is the useful information that explains how to read and use a map. Below is a short summary of each type of information found on a map. Not understanding the marginal information on a map can lead to serious errors while navigating.

**Sheet Name.** The sheet name is found in bold print at the center of the top and in the lower left area of the map margin. A map is generally named for the largest settlement contained within the area covered by the sheet, or for the largest natural feature located within the area at the time the map was drawn.

**Sheet Number.** The sheet number is found in bold print in both the upper right and lower left areas of the margin, and in the center box of the adjoining sheets diagram, which is found in the lower right margin. It is used as a reference number to link specific maps to overlays, operations orders, and plans.

**Series Name.** The map series name is found in bold print in the upper left corner of the margin. The name given to the series is generally that of a major political subdivision such as a state within the United States or a European nation. A map series usually includes a group of similar maps at the same scale and on the same sheet lines or format designed to cover a particular geographic area. It may also be a group of maps that serve a common purpose such as the military city maps.

**Scale.** The scale is found both in the upper left margin after the series name, and in the center of the lower margin. The scale note is a representative fraction that gives the ratio of a map distance to the corresponding distance on the earth's surface. For example, the scale note 1:50,000 indicates that one unit of measure on the map equals 50,000 units of the same measure on the ground. 1:50,000 is the most commonly used military map scale.

**Series Number.** The series number is found in both the upper right margin and the lower left margin. It is a sequence reference expressed either as a four-digit numeral (1234) or as a letter, followed by a three- or four-digit numeral (M123, T5678).

**Edition Number.** The edition number is found in bold print in the upper right area of the top margin and the lower left area of the bottom margin. Editions are numbered consecutively; therefore, if you have more than one edition, the highest numbered sheet is the most recent. Most military maps are now published by the NGA, but older editions of maps may have been produced by the U.S. Army Map Service. Still others may have been drawn, at least in part, by the U.S. Army Corps of Engineers, the U.S. Geological Survey, or other agencies affiliated or not with the United States or allied governments. The credit line, telling who produced the map, is just above the legend. The map information date is found immediately below the word "LEGEND" in the lower left margin of the map. This date is important when determining how accurately the map data might be expected to match what you will encounter on the ground.

**Index to Boundaries.** The index to boundaries diagram appears in the lower or right margin of all sheets. This diagram, which is a miniature of the map, shows the boundaries that occur within the map area such as county lines and state boundaries.

**Adjoining Sheets Diagram.** Maps at all standard scales contain a diagram that illustrates the adjoining sheets. On maps at 1:100,000 and larger scales and at 1:1,000,000 scale, the diagram is called the index to adjoining sheets. It consists of as many rectangles representing adjoining sheets as are necessary to surround the rectangle that represents the sheet under consideration. The diagram usually contains nine rectangles, but the number may vary depending on the locations of the adjoining sheets. All represented sheets are identified by their sheet numbers. Sheets of an adjoining series, whether published or planned, that are at the same scale are represented by dashed lines. The series number of the adjoining series is indicated along the appropriate side of the division line between the series.

**Elevation Guide.** The elevation guide is normally found in the lower right margin. It is a miniature characterization of the terrain shown. The terrain is represented by bands of elevation, spot elevations, and major drainage features. The elevation guide provides the map reader with a means of quick recognition of major landforms.

**Declination Diagram.** The declination diagram is located in the lower margin of large-scale maps and indicates the angular relationships of true north, grid north, and magnetic north. On maps at 1:250,000 scale, this information is expressed as a note in the lower margin. In recent edition maps, there is a note indicating the conversion of azimuths from grid to magnetic and from magnetic to grid next to the declination diagram.

**Bar Scales.** Bar scales are located in the center of the lower margin. They are rulers used to convert map distance to ground distance. Maps have three or more bar scales, each in a different unit of measure. Care should be exercised when using the scales, especially in the selection of the unit of measure that is needed.

**Contour Interval Note.** The contour interval note is found in the center of the lower margin normally below the bar scales. It states the vertical distance between adjacent contour lines of the map. When supplementary contours are used, the interval is indicated. In recent edition maps, the contour interval is given in meters instead of feet. You will want to pay special attention to this when using an unfamiliar map to get an idea of the terrain you will be facing.

**Spheroid Note.** The spheroid note is located in the center of the lower margin. Spheriods (ellipsoids) have specific parameters that define the X Y Z axis of the earth. The spheriod is an integral part of the datum.

**Grid Note.** The grid note is located in the center of the lower margin. It gives information pertaining to the grid system used and the interval between grid lines, and it identifies the UTM grid zone number.

**Projection Note.** The projection system is the framework of the map. For military maps, this framework is of the conformal type; that is, small areas of the surface of the earth retain their true shapes on the projection; measured angles closely approximate true values; and the scale factor is the same in all directions from a point. The projection note is located in the center of the lower margin. (Refer to NGA for the development characteristics of the conformal-type projection systems.)

**Vertical Datum Note.** The vertical datum note is located in the center of the lower margin. The vertical datum or vertical-control datum is defined as any level surface taken as a surface of reference from which to determine elevations. In the United States, Canada, and Europe, the vertical datum refers to the mean sea level surface. However, in parts of Asia and Africa, the vertical-control datum may vary locally and is based on an assumed elevation that has no connection to any sea level surface.

Map readers should habitually check the vertical datum note on maps, particularly if the map is used for lowlevel aircraft navigation, naval gunfire support, or missile target acquisition.

**Horizontal Datum Note.** The horizontal datum note is located in the center of the lower margin. The horizontal datum or horizontal-control datum is defined as a geodetic reference point (of which five quantities are known: latitude, longitude, azimuth of a line from this point, and two constants, which are the parameters of reference ellipsoid). These are the basis for horizontal-control surveys. The horizontal-control datum may extend over a continent or be limited to a small local area. Maps and charts produced by NGA are produced on 32 different horizontal-control data. Map readers should habitually check the horizontal datum note on every map or chart, especially adjacent map sheets, to ensure the products are based on the same horizontal datum. If products are based on different horizontal-control data, coordinate transformations to a common datum must be performed. UTM coordinates from the same point computed on different data may differ as much as 900 meters.

**Control Note.** The control note is located in the center of the lower margin. It indicates the special agencies involved in the control of the technical aspects of all the information that is disseminated on the map.

**Preparation Note.** The preparation note is located in the center of the lower margin. It indicates the agency responsible for preparing the map.

**Printing Note.** The printing note is also located in the center of the lower margin. It indicates the agency responsible for printing the map and the date the map was printed. The printing data should not be used to determine when the map information was obtained.

**Grid Reference Box.** The grid reference box is normally located in the center of the lower margin. It contains instructions for composing a grid reference.

**Unit Imprint and Symbol.** The unit imprint and symbol is on the left side of the lower margin. It identifies the agency that prepared and printed the map with its respective symbol. This information is important to the map user in evaluating the reliability of the map.

**Legend.** The legend is located in the lower left margin. It illustrates and identifies the topographic symbols used to depict some of the more prominent features on the map. The symbols are not always the same on every map. Always refer to the legend to avoid errors when reading a map.

**ADDITIONAL NOTES:** Not all maps contain the same items of marginal information. Under certain conditions, special notes and scales may be added to aid the map user.

**Glossary.** The glossary is an explanation of technical terms or a translation of terms on maps of foreign areas where the native language is other than English.

**Classification.** Certain maps require a note indicating the security classification. This is shown in the upper and lower margins.

**Protractor Scale.** The protractor scale may appear in the upper margin on some maps. It is used to lay out the magnetic-grid declination for the map, which, in turn, is used to orient the map sheet with the aid of the lensatic compass.

**Coverage Diagram.** On maps at scales of 1:100,000 and larger, a coverage diagram may be used. It is normally in the lower or right margin and indicates the methods by which the map was made, dates of photography, and reliability of the sources. On maps at 1:250,000 scale, the coverage diagram is replaced by a reliability diagram.

**Special Notes.** A special note is any statement of general information that relates to the mapped area. It is normally found in the lower right margin. For example: This map is red-light readable.

**User's Note.** The user's note is normally located in the lower right-hand margin. It requests cooperation in correcting errors or omissions on the map. Errors should be marked and the map forwarded to the agency identified in the note.

**Stock Number Identification.** All maps published by the NGA that are in the Department of the Army map supply system contain stock number identifications that are used in requisitioning map supplies. The identification consists of the words "STOCK NO" followed by a unique designation that is composed of the series number, the sheet number of the individual map and, on recently printed sheets, the edition number. The designation is limited to 15 units (letters and numbers). The first 5 units are allotted to the series number; when the series number is less than 5 units, the letter "X" is substituted as the fifth unit. The sheet number is the next component; however, Roman numerals, which are part of the sheet number, are converted to Arabic numerals in the stock number. The last 2 units are the edition number; the first digit of the edition number is a zero if the number is less than 10. If the current edition number is unknown, the number 01 is used. The latest available edition will be furnished. Asterisks are placed between the sheet number and the edition number when necessary to ensure there are at least 11 units in the stock number.

**Conversion Graph.** Normally found in the right margin, the conversion graph indicates the conversion of different units of measure used on the map.

BASICS

## COLOR ON A MAP
**There are 6 colors on a military map.**

- Black - Man made features other than roads
- Blue - Water
- Brown - All relief features: contour lines on old maps, cultivated land on red light readable maps
- Green - Vegetation
- Red - Major roads, built up areas, special features on old maps
- Red-Brown - All relief features and main roads on red-light readable maps

## TERRAIN FEATURES
There are 8 terrain features that you need to learn what they look like on a map and when standing on them. 5 are considered major terrain features and 3 are considered minor terrain features.

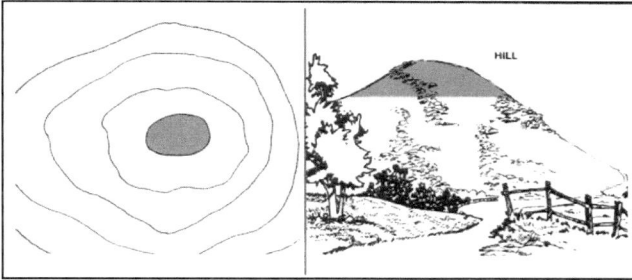

## Major Terrain Features

**Hill-** A point or small area of high ground from which the ground slopes down in all directions. On a map it is indicated by contour lines forming concentric circles.

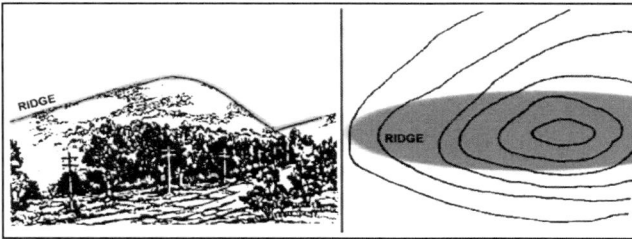

**Ridge-** A line of high ground with height variations along its crest. Contour lines forming a U or V; closed end points away from high ground.

**Valley-** Reasonably level ground bordered on the sides by higher ground. Usually has maneuver room and contains a stream. Contour lines form a U. Lines tend to parallel stream before crossing. Contour line crossing a stream always points upstream.

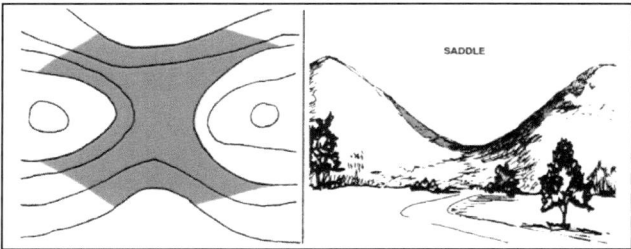

**Saddle-** A dip or low point along a ridge crest; either lower ground between two hill tops or a break in the crest. A saddle is normally represented by an hourglass contour line shape.

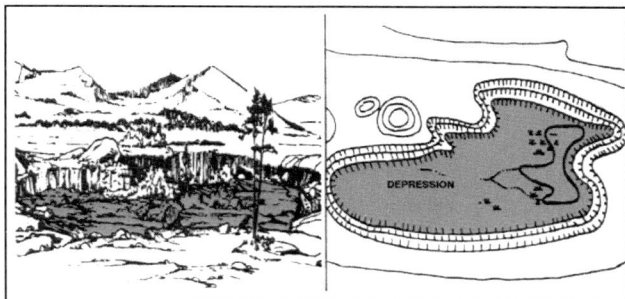

**Depression-** Low point or hole in the ground with higher ground on all sides. Indicated by closed contour lines that have tick marks pointing toward the low ground.

## MINOR TERRAIN FEATURES

**Draw-** Like a valley, but normally has less developed stream course. No level ground and little or no maneuver room. Ground slopes upward on the sides and toward the head of the draw. Contour lines are V-shaped with the point of the V toward the head of the draw (high ground).

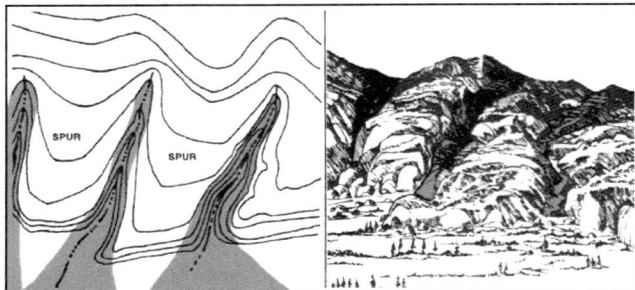

**Spur-** Short, continuously sloping line of higher ground jutting out the side of a ridge. Often formed by parallel streams cutting draws down a ridge. Contour lines depict a spur with the U or V pointing away from high ground.

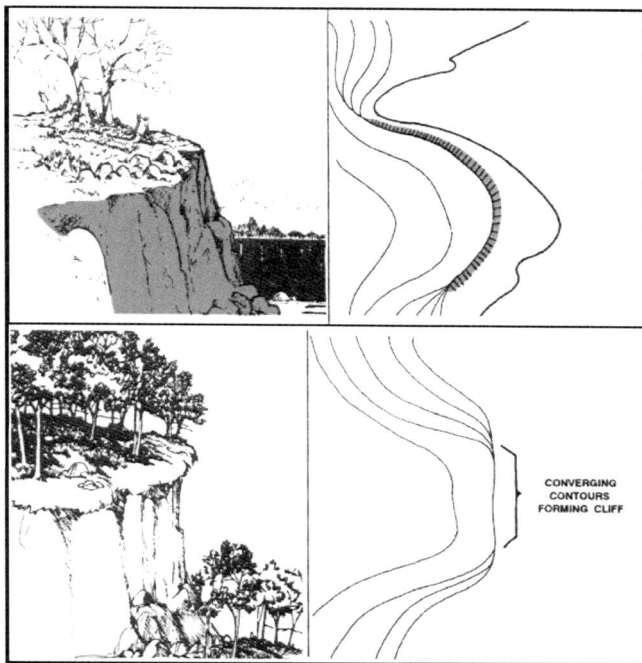

CONVERGING
CONTOURS
FORMING CLIFF

Cliff- A vertical or near vertical slope. Contour lines are very close together.

Below is an example of how you can use your hand
to illustrate the terrain features:

ILLUSTRATING TERRAIN FEATURES BY HAND

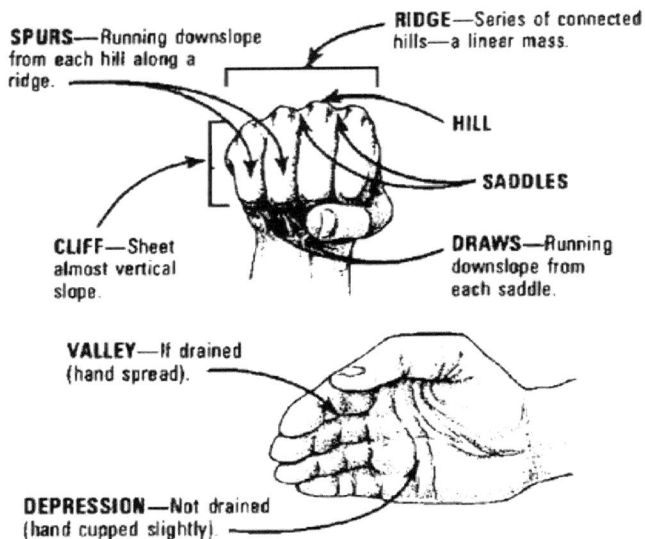

SPURS—Running downslope
from each hill along a
ridge.

RIDGE—Series of connected
hills—a linear mass.

HILL

SADDLES

CLIFF—Sheet
almost vertical
slope.

DRAWS—Running
downslope from
each saddle.

VALLEY—If drained
(hand spread).

DEPRESSION—Not drained
(hand cupped slightly).

# CHAPTER 2:
# DISTANCE

## STRAIGHT LINE
Measuring distance on a map is critical to be able to determine how far you must travel between points or locations. You can measure straight line distance and curved distance (roads).

The most accurate method for measuring **straight line distance** on a map is to line up a straight edge of a piece of paper (or 3x5 card) and mark your start and end point on the paper. Then match up the paper with the appropriate bar scale on the bottom of the map. Ensure you use the bar scale for meters!

Another method for measuring straight line distance is to mark the start and end points on a sheet of paper and use the 1/50,000 meter coordinate scale triangle inside your protractor to measure the straight line distance.

## CURVED DISTANCE
**Measuring curved distance** is important when travelling mounted. The most accurate way to measure road distance is to use the straight edge of a sheet of paper and place a mark at your starting point. Place another mark on the paper at the first curve in the road you come to. Rotate the blank paper to follow the road, placing a tick mark at each curve.

Once you have completed this, simply measure the total distance between your first and last tick mark on the sheet of paper using your bar scale.

## BAR SCALES

**The bar scales** will be located at the bottom of the map. Generally any distance on paper of 1 inch equals 1,000 meters. Most maps have 4 different bar scales in meters, statue miles, yards, and nautical miles. For all dismounted movements you will want to use the meter bar scale. Sometimes for mounted movements you might want to use the miles bar chart, particularly if your vehicle has an odometer.

# CHAPTER 3:
# GRID COORDINATES

## HOW TO USE A PROTRACTOR

Determining grid coordinates is the absolute most important fundamental of land navigation. If you screw up plotting your point on a Land Nav course, you will never find it! Before you can begin to plot a point on a map, you must be able to use a protractor.

The military protractor, GTA 5-2-12, contains two scales: one in degrees (inner scale) and one in mils (outer scale). This protractor represents the azimuth circle. The degree scale is graduated from 0 to 360 degrees; each tick mark on the degree scale represents one degree. A line from 0 to 180 degrees is called the base line of the protractor. Where the base line intersects the horizontal line, between 90 and 270 degrees, is the index or center of the protractor.

When using the protractor, the base line is always oriented parallel to a north-south grid line. The 0- or 360- degree mark is always toward the top or north on the map and the 90° mark is to the right.

On the 1:50,000 coordinate scale (upper left of the protractor), there are two sides: vertical and horizontal. These sides are 1,000 meters in length. The point at which the sides meet is the zero-zero point. Each side is divided into 10 equal 100-meter segments by a long tick mark and number. Each 100-meter segment is subdivided into 50-meter segments by a short tick mark. By using interpolation, mentally divide each 50-meter segment into tenths. For example, a point that lies after a whole number but before a short tick mark is identified as 10, 20, 30, or 40 meters and any point that lies after the short tick mark but before the whole number is identified as 60, 70, 80, or 90 meters.

To ensure the scale is correctly aligned, place it with the zero-zero point at the lower left corner of the grid square. Keeping the horizontal line of the scale directly on top of the east-west grid line, slide the scale to the right until the vertical line of the scale touches the point for which the coordinates are desired. Remember to always ready RIGHT and then Up!

Coordinates are written as one continuous number without spaces, parentheses, dashes, or decimal points; they must always contain an even number of digits. Therefore, whoever is to use the written coordinates must know where to make the split between the RIGHT and UP readings. It is a military requirement that the 100,000-meter square identification letters be included in any point designation. Normally, grid coordinates are determined to the nearest 100 meters (six digits) for reporting locations. With practice, this can be done without using plotting scales. The location of targets and points on land navigation courses are determined to the nearest 10 meters (eight digits).

## 4, 6, AND 8 DIGIT GRID

There is only one rule to remember when reading or reporting grid coordinates— always read to the RIGHT and then UP. The first half of the reported set of coordinate digits represents the left-to-right (easting) grid label, and the second half represents the label as read from the bottom to top (northing). The grid coordinates may represent the location to the nearest 10-, 100-, or 1,000-meter increment.

**NOTE:** Special care should be exercised when recording and reporting coordinates. Transposing numbers or making errors could be detrimental to military operations.

The precision of a point's location is shown by the number of digits in the coordinates; the more digits, the more precise the location.

# NOTES:

# CHAPTER 4:
# LOCATE YOUR POSITION

## DETERMINE A LOCATION ON THE GROUND BY TERRAIN ASSOCIATION

A map can be oriented by terrain association when a compass is not available or when the user has to make many quick references as he moves across country. Using this method requires careful examination of the map and the ground, and the user must know his approximate location.

The first step to determine your location on the ground is to determine what type of terrain feature you are located on. Then determine what types of terrain features surround your location. Next, you want to orient your map. Determine the four cardinal directions (North, South, East, and West).
Determine your location.

   a. Relate the terrain features on the ground to those shown on the map.
   b. After you have determined where the terrain features on the ground and those on the map coincide, determine the coordinates of your location using the coordinate scale and protractor.

The technique of moving by terrain association is more forgiving of mistakes and far less time-consuming than dead reckoning. It best suits those situations that call for movement from one area to another. Errors made using terrain association are easily corrected because you are comparing what you expected to see from the map to what you do see on the ground. Errors are anticipated and will not go unchecked. You can easily make adjustments based upon what you encounter. Periodic position-fixing through either plotted or estimated resection will also make it possible to correct your movements, call for fire, or call in the locations of enemy targets or any other information of tactical or logistical importance.

Using terrain association is much like giving/following directions. When someone tells you where they live it might sound like this: "Go West until you come to the Super Wal-Mart and then bang a left. Keep the river on your right hand side and go through 3 lights. Turn right at the 4th light and my house is on the left. If you come to the bridge you have gone too far."

That is exactly how you navigate using terrain association. You know the general direction you want to go and you have checkpoints along the way so you know you are continuing in the right direction. You utilize handrails wherever possible and try to have a backstop in the event you overshoot your point or objective.

The best way to learn terrain association is to see different terrain on the ground and compare it to a map. Terrain features are different on the ground, but they all have the same characteristics. The better you get at recognizing terrain features on the ground, the better you will become at terrain association.

## ORIENT YOUR MAP

The first step for a navigator in the field is orienting the map. A map is oriented when it is in a horizontal position with its north and south corresponding to the north and south on the ground.

Some orienting techniques follow:

**Using a Compass.** When orienting a map with a compass, remember that the compass measures magnetic azimuths. Since the magnetic arrow points to magnetic north, pay special attention to the declination diagram. There are two techniques used.

**First Technique.** Determine the direction of the declination and its value from the declination diagram.

With the map in a horizontal position, take the straightedge on the left side of the compass and place it alongside the north-south grid line with the cover of the compass pointing toward the top of the map. This procedure places the fixed black index line of the compass parallel to north-south grid lines of the map.

Keeping the compass aligned as directed above, rotate the map and compass together until the magnetic arrow is below the fixed black index line on the compass. At this time, the map is close to being oriented.

Rotate the map and compass in the direction of the declination diagram.

If the magnetic north arrow on the map is to the left of the grid north, check the compass reading to see if it equals the G-M angle given in the declination diagram. The map is then oriented (See figure below).

ORIENTING MAP WITH COMPASS, A-1

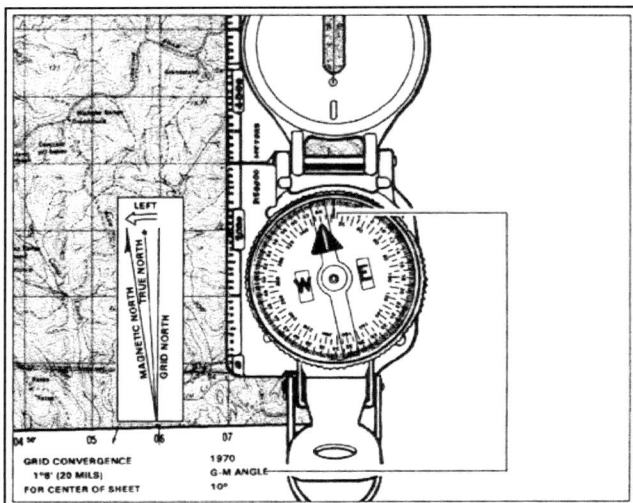

If the magnetic north is to the right of grid north, check the compass reading to see if it equals 360 degrees minus the G-M angle (See figure below).

ORIENTING MAP WITH COMPASS, A-2

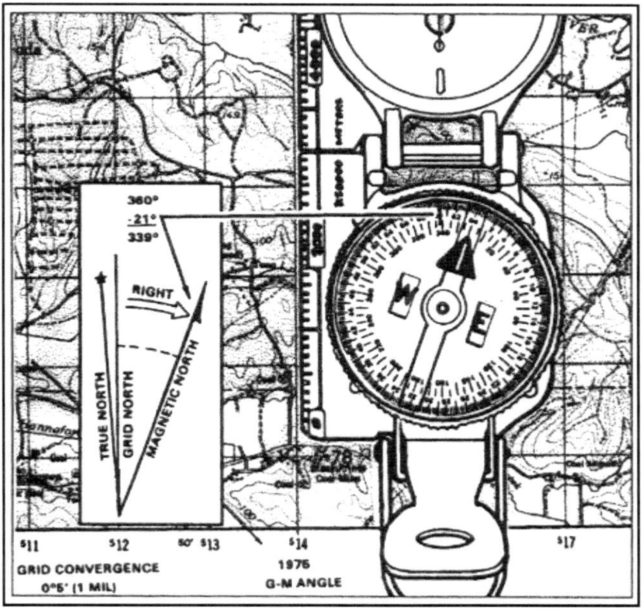

**Second Technique.** Determine the direction of the declination and its value from the declination diagram.

Using any north-south grid line on the map as a base, draw a magnetic azimuth equal to the G-M angle given in the declination diagram with the protractor.

If the declination is easterly (right), the drawn line is equal to the value of the G-M angle. Then align the straightedge, which is on the left side of the compass, alongside the drawn line on the map. Rotate the map and compass until the magnetic arrow of the compass is below the fixed black index line. The map is now oriented (See figure below).

ORIENTING MAP WITH COMPASS, A-3

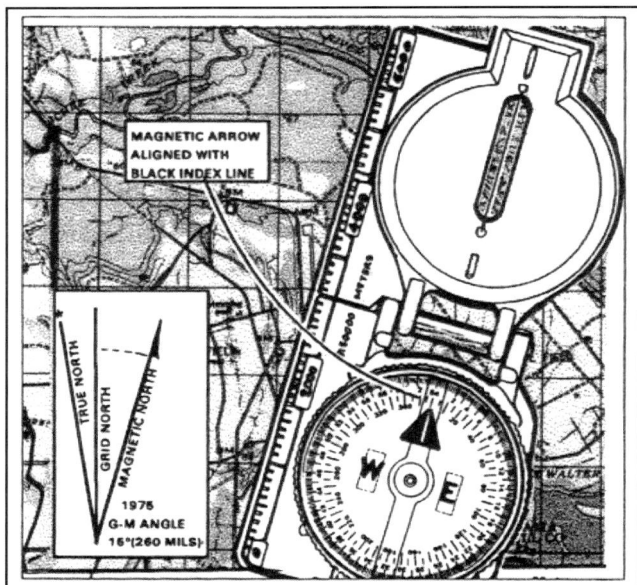

If the declination is westerly (left), the drawn line will equal 360 degrees minus the value of the G-M angle. Then align the straightedge, which is on the left side of the compass, alongside the drawn line on the map. Rotate the map and compass until the magnetic arrow of the compass is below the fixed black index line. The map is now oriented (See below figure).

**NOTE:** Once the map is oriented, magnetic azimuths are determined using the compass. Do not move the map from its oriented position since any change in its position moves it out of line with the magnetic north.

Special care should be taken whenever orienting your map with a compass. A small mistake can cause you to navigate in the wrong direction.

## Intersection

Intersection is the location of an unknown point by successively occupying at least two (preferably three) known positions on the ground and then map sighting on the unknown location. It is used to locate distant or inaccessible points or objects such as enemy targets and danger areas. There are two methods of intersection: the map and compass method and the straightedge method.

When using the **map and compass method**—
- Orient the map using the compass.
- Locate and mark your position on the map
- Determine the magnetic azimuth to the unknown position using the compass.
- Convert the magnetic azimuth to grid azimuth.
- Draw a line on the map from your position on this grid azimuth.
- Move to a second known point and repeat steps 1, 2, 3, 4, and 5.
- The location of the unknown position is where the lines cross on the map. Determine the grid coordinates to the desired accuracy.

**The straight edge method** is used when a compass is not available. When using it—
- Orient the map on a flat surface by the terrain association method.
- Locate and mark your position on the map.
- Lay a straight edge on the map with one end at the user's position as a pivot point; then, rotate the straightedge until the unknown point is sighted along the edge.
- Draw a line along the straight edge
- Repeat the above steps at the next position and check for accuracy.
- The intersection of the lines on the map is the location of the unknown point. Determine the grid coordinates to the desired accuracy.

## Resection

Resection is the method of locating one's position on a map by determining the grid azimuth to at least two well defined locations that can be pinpointed on the map. For greater accuracy, the desired method of resection would be to use three or more well-defined locations.

When using the **map and compass method**—

- Orient the map using the compass.
- Identify two or three known distant locations on the ground and mark them on the map.
- Measure the magnetic azimuth to one of the known positions from your location using a compass.
- Convert the magnetic azimuth to a grid azimuth.
- Convert the grid azimuth to a back azimuth.
- Using a protractor, draw a line for the back azimuth on the map from the known position back toward your unknown position.
- Repeat 3, 4, and 5 for a second position and a third position, if desired.
- The intersection of the lines is your location. Determine the grid coordinates to the desired accuracy.

When using the **straightedge method**—

- Orient the map on a flat surface by the terrain association method.
- Locate at least two known distant locations or prominent features on the ground and mark them on the map.
- Lay a straightedge on the map using a known position as a pivot point. Rotate the straightedge until the known position on the map is aligned with the known position on the ground.
- Draw a line along the straightedge away from the known position on the ground toward your position.
- Repeat 3 and 4 using a second known position.
- The intersection of the lines on the map is your location. Determine the grid coordinates to the desired accuracy.

## POLAR COORDINATES

A method of locating or plotting an unknown position from a known point by giving a direction and a distance along that direction line is called polar coordinates. The following elements must be present when using polar coordinates:

-Present Known Location on a map
-Azimuth (grid or magnetic)
-Distance in meters

# CHAPTER 5:
# USE A COMPASS

## LENSATIC

The **lensatic compass** is the most commonly used compass in the military. The floating dial is used to determine the direction in which you are pointing your compass. The outer black ring of numbers and tick marks are used for finding direction in mils. The inner red ring of numbers and tick marks are used for finding direction in degrees. On all land nav courses do not confuse the mils and degrees while navigating the course!

### DIAGRAM OF A LENSATIC COMPASS

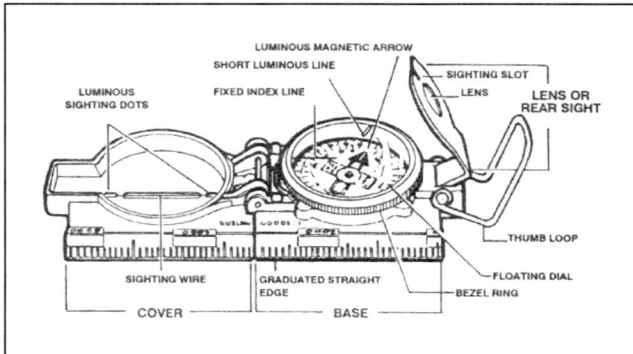

There are 360 degrees or 6400 mils in a circle. These are marked with a tick mark every 5 degrees or 20 mils.

To read direction, point the compass in the direction you
want to go or want to determine. Look beneath the index
line on the outer glass cover and estimate to the nearest
degree the position of the index line over the red scale. Be
careful to hold the compass still so that the dial remains
stationary while you are reading the scale.

The arrow on your compass points toward magnetic
north. The arrow is also attracted to any metal objects;
for example, a truck, your rifle, your helmet, and electrical
power lines. Ensure your compass is away from any metal
objects so you don't get a false reading.

There are two methods to holding a lensatic compass:
The compass to cheek method and the center hold method.

To use the **compass to cheek method**, open the cover
of the compass to a 90 degree angle and position the eye
piece at a 45 degree angle. Place your thumb through
the thumb loop on the compass, form a steady base with
your third and fourth fingers and extend your index
finger along the side of the compass base.

Place the hand holding the compass into the palm of
the other hand. Bring both hands up to your face and
position the thumb that is through the loop against your
cheekbone. Look through the lens of the eyepiece. If the
dial is not in focus, move the eyepiece up or down until
the dial is in focus. Align the sighting slot of the eyepiece
with the sighting wire in the cover on the point for which
the azimuth is being determined. Look through the lens
of the eyepiece and read the azimuth under the index line.

To use the **center-hold method** open the compass so that the cover forms a straight edge with the base. The lens of the compass is moved out of the way. Next, place your thumb through the loop, form a steady base with your third and fourth fingers, and extend your index finger along the side of the compass. Place the thumb of the other hand between the eyepiece and lens, extend the index finger along the other side of the compass, wrap your remaining fingers around the fingers of the other hand, and pull your elbows firmly into your side. This will place the compass between your chin and your belt.

To measure an azimuth, turn your entire body toward the object and point the compass cover directly at the object. Look down and read the azimuth from beneath the fixed black index line. This method can also be used at night.

The center-hold method is used when you don't have to have a precise azimuth. It is also the most commonly used method on Army land nav courses. Stop occasionally to check the azimuth along which you are moving. Also, you can move from object to object along your path by shooting an azimuth to each object and then moving to that object.

USE A COMPASS

## M2 ARTILLERY COMPASS

**The M2 Artillery compass** is a rustproof and dustproof magnetic instrument that provides slope, angle of site, and azimuth readings. One of the most important features of the M2 compass is that it is graduated in mils and does not require a conversion from degrees to mils as does the M1 compass. It can be calibrated to provide a grid azimuth or it can be used uncalibrated to determine a magnetic azimuth.

### M2 ARTILLERY COMPASS

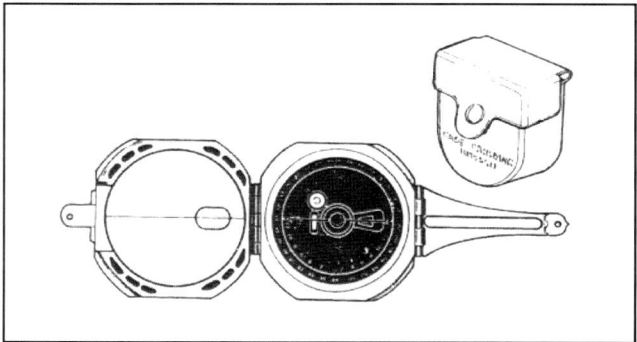

Except for the magnetic needle and its pivot, the compass is made of nonmagnetic materials. When the cover is closed, the magnetic needle is automatically lifted from its pivot and held firmly against the glass window. When the compass is open and leveled, the needle floats freely upon its pivot and points to magnetic north. Note that both ends of the needle are shaped like an arrow, and that one arrow is painted white and the other is black. It is the white end of the needle that points to magnetic north. Because the needle is magnetic, it will also be attracted to large iron or steel objects in the near vicinity, to electrical power lines, and to operating generators. Magnetic compass readings measured near such objects are apt to be in error due to the magnetic attraction of these objects.

The M2 compass has a **circular level** that is used to level the instrument when measuring azimuths. The circular level bubble must be centered before reading the azimuth. The compass is equipped with front and rear sights for aligning on the object to which the azimuth is desired.

The **compass azimuth scale** is a circle divided into 6400 mils. Beginning with zero, the graduations are numbered every 200 mils. The long, unnumbered graduations appearing halfway between the numbered graduations are the odd-numbered hundreds (100, 300, 500, and so forth). Short graduation marks divide each 100-mil segment into equal portions of 20 mils.

**Reading the Azimuth Scale.** Azimuths are read from the azimuth scale from the black end of the compass needle.

**Setting Up the Compass.** To set up the M2 compass, open the cover and fold the rear sight holder out parallel with the face of the compass. Fold the rear sight up, perpendicular with its holder. Fold the front sight up, parallel with the mirror. Then fold the cover (mirror) toward the compass until it is at an angle of approximately 45 degrees to the face of the compass so that, with your eye behind the rear sight, the black end of the compass needle can be readily viewed in the mirror. The compass is now set up for measuring an azimuth.

**Measuring an Azimuth.** Once the compass is set up and all steel objects are at least 18 meters away from your position, you are ready to measure an azimuth. Hold the compass in both hands at eye level with your arms braced against your body and with the rear sight nearest your eyes. Sight through the rear sight and the window in the mirror and align the hairline at the reflection of the face of the compass. Center the circular level bubble. With the bubble centered and the hairline aligned on the object, look at the mirror reflection of the compass scale and read the azimuth to which the black end of the needle is pointing. Remember, magnetic attractions or movement by you may cause errors in your readings.

# CHAPTER 6:
# AZIMUTH CONVERSION

## CONVERT A GRID AZIMUTH TO MAGNETIC

Soldiers need a way of expressing direction that is accurate and universal. Because of this, direction is expressed as a unit of angular measure. The most common unit of measure is the degree. In order to measure something, there must always be a starting point or zero measurement. To express direction as a unit of angular measure, there must be a starting point or zero measure and a point of reference. These two points designate the base or reference line. There are three base lines— true north, magnetic north, and grid north. The most commonly used are magnetic and grid.

**True North.** A line from any point on the earth's surface to the north pole. All lines of longitude are true north lines. True north is usually represented by a star.

**Magnetic North.** The direction to the north magnetic pole, as indicated by the north-seeking needle of a magnetic instrument. The magnetic north is usually symbolized by a line ending with half of an arrowhead. Magnetic readings are obtained with magnetic instruments, such as lensatic and M2 compasses.

## Convert a Magnetic Azimuth to Grid

**Grid North.** The north that is established by using the vertical grid lines on the map. Grid north may be symbolized by the letters GN or the letter "y."

There is an angular difference between the grid north and the magnetic north. Since the location of magnetic north does not correspond exactly with the grid-north lines on the maps, a conversion from magnetic to grid or vice versa is needed.

The G-M angle value is the angular size that exists between grid north and magnetic north. It is an arc, indicated by a dashed line that connects the grid-north and magnetic-north prongs. This value is expressed to the nearest 1/2 degree, with mil equivalents shown to the nearest 10 mils. The G-M angle is important to the map reader/land navigator because azimuths translated between map and ground will be in error by the size of the declination angle if not adjusted for it.

Simply refer to the conversion notes that appear in conjunction with the diagram explaining the use of the G-M angle. One note provides instructions for converting magnetic azimuth to grid azimuth; the other, for converting grid azimuth to magnetic azimuth. The conversion (add or subtract) is governed by the direction of the magnetic-north prong relative to that of the north-grid prong.

## NORTHS

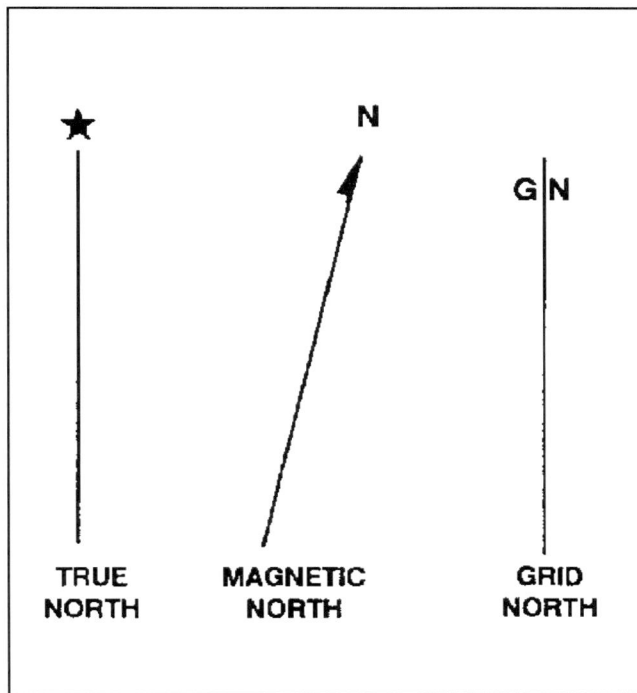

## Use a Declination Diagram

Declination is the angular difference between any two norths. If you have a map and a compass, the one of most interest to you will be between magnetic and grid north. The declination diagram shows the angular relationship, represented by prongs, among grid, magnetic, and true norths. While the relative positions of the prongs are correct, they are seldom plotted to scale. Do not use the diagram to measure a numerical value. This value will be written in the map margin (in both degrees and mils) beside the diagram.

### Declination Diagram

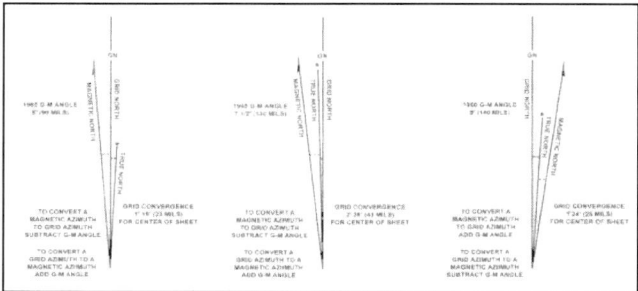

**STOP!!!!** On every land nav course you do, make sure you check the declination diagram and convert your grid azimuths to magnetic azimuths before leaving your start point!

When working with allied Soldiers, like the Brits or Canadians, they will use the term **"bearing,"** but it is the same as an azimuth.

# CHAPTER 7:
# NAVIGATE

## NAVIGATE DISMOUNTED

The ability to navigate dismounted is the most critical skill in order to pass Ranger School, SFAS, Delta Selection, and all officer and NCO basic and advanced courses. Land navigation, like speaking a foreign language, is a perishable skill. If it is not practiced and skills kept sharp, you lose proficiency.

Before you can begin to navigate dismounted, you must first know where you are located. Most courses will give you an 8 digit grid coordinate for your starting point or it is a major terrain feature or road intersection. Plot this point on your map and beside the point write "SP" for start point and circle it so you don't confuse it with your other points. Once you have plotted your start point, recheck it.

Next you have to know where you are going. Most traditional land nav courses will give you a list of all of your points. You will want to take your time and plot each point carefully then go back and recheck to make sure they are plotted correctly. Make as small of a dot as possible. The finer lead in the pencil the better. A #2 pencil creates too large of a dot.

Once all of your points are plotted correctly it is time to do your route selection. This is the order in which you will go to each point. You won't necessarily want to go in the order the points were listed on your paper. You want to choose your route based on trying to cover the least amount of distance while taking the terrain into consideration as well. I like to choose a route with good checkpoints along the way. The best checkpoints are linear running features that cross your route such as streams, roads, power lines, ridges, or valleys. These will allow you to stay on your route easily.

Sometimes I don't navigate right to the point but rather navigate to an attack point. If the point is several hundred meters from an intersection then I will navigate to that intersection, go into the woods 20 meters and shoot an azimuth and dead reckon from my attack point to the point. This is why your map analysis for your route selection is so critical.

It is also good to identify a backstop. A backstop is a feature beyond your point, where if you come to it then you know you have gone too far passed your point. The best backstops are hard top roads if possible.

After you have selected your route, you need to get your azimuths and distances. Ensure you check the declination diagram to see if you need to convert your grid azimuth to a magnetic azimuth. Make sure you are accurate when measuring your distances you have to travel. The key is having a good pace count! You must know your pace count when walking cross country or through the woods. Also, if you know the land nav course requires you to wear a rucksack with a set weight, then you need to get your pace count wearing the prescribed weight. It will be much different than your pace count with just an LCE or MOLLE vest on.

As you navigate dismounted on a test course, I recommend using a hybrid of dead reckoning and terrain association. You should dead reckon by staying on azimuth and keeping up with your pace count, but also be aware of the terrain as you go, by having check-points, attack points, and backstops. I am a big fan of handrailing whenever possible. Handrailing is when you have a road, trail or stream that you can walk parallel with. You will need to stay at least 20 meters into the woods but this technique will allow you to move quickly without much compass work. You just have to realize if your handrail heads in a different direction you will have to part ways with it.

Before you leave each point, double check your map to ensure you are using the correct azimuth and pace count for the next point. Never lay your weapon or rucksack down while you search for a point. You will not be able to find them. Try to avoid real thick vegetation and streams without ford sites.

Make sure you adhere to all rules of the land nav course. The two big ones that get students kicked out are talking to other students and sleeping on the course.

NAVIGATE

Some courses allow you to walk the trails, but be careful because not all of the trails are on the map.

Remember the course is timed so you need to move with a purpose, but don't injure yourself. You should be able to walk the majority of a land nav course and still make it in plenty of time.

## Navigate Mounted

The principles for mounted navigation are the same as dismounted, but the primary difference is speed of travel. It might take you two hours on foot to get to a location that will only take you 20 minutes mounted. To be effective at mounted navigation, the travel speed must always be considered.

The navigator should not be given any other duties and the leader should never be the navigator. Before departing, the navigator should ensure he has all the tools to navigate: map, compass, pencil, protractor, etc. When mounted, a map board is very effective.

When preparing to move, the effects of terrain on navigating mounted vehicles must be determined. You will cover great distances very quickly, and you must develop the ability to estimate the distance you have traveled. Remember that 0.1 mile is roughly 160 meters, and 1 mile is about 1,600 meters or 1.6 kms. Having a mobility advantage helps while navigating. Mobility makes it much easier if you get disoriented to move to a point where you can reorient yourself.

NAVIGATE

**NOTE:** To convert kmph to mph, multiply by .62.
(9 kmph x .62 = 5.58 mph). To convert mph to kmph,
divide mph by .62 (10 mph 0.62 = 16.12 kmph).

When determining a route to be used when mounted,
consider the capabilities of the vehicles to be used. Most
military vehicles are limited in the degree of slope they
can climb and the type of terrain they can negotiate.
Swamps, thickly wooded areas, or deep streams may
present no problems to dismounted soldiers, but the
same terrain may completely stop mounted soldiers.
The navigator must consider this when selecting a route.

Weather can halt mounted movement. Snow and ice are
obvious dangers, but more significant is the effect of
rain and snow on soil load-bearing ability. Cross country
vehicles may be restricted to road movement in heavy
rain. If it has rained recently, adjust your route to avoid
flooded or muddy areas. A mired vehicle only
hinders combat capability.

Locate the start point and finish point on the map.
Determine the map's grid azimuth from start point
to finish point and convert it to a magnetic azimuth.
Determine the distance between the start point and
finish point or any intermediate points on the map
and make a thorough map reconnaissance of that area.

Terrain association is the most widely used method
of navigation. The navigator plans his route so that
he moves from terrain feature to terrain feature. An

NAVIGATE

automobile driver in a city uses this technique as he moves along a street or series of streets, guiding on intersections or features such as stores and parks. Like the driver, the navigator selects routes or streets between key points or *intersections*. These routes must be capable of sustaining the travel of the vehicle or vehicles, should be relatively direct, and should be easy to follow. In a typical move, the navigator determines his location, determines the location of his objective, notes the position of both on his map, and then selects a route between the two.

Use a Logbook. When the routes have been selected and the navigator has divided the distance to be traveled into legs, prepare a logbook. The logbook is an informal record of the distance and azimuth of each leg, with notes to aid the navigator in following the correct route. The notes list easily identifiable terrain features at or near the point where the direction of movement changes.

## LOGBOOK EXAMPLE

| ODOMETER READING AT START | ODOMETER READING AT FINISH | DISTANCE IN MILES | AZIMUTH | DEVIATION CORRECTION | NOTES |
|---|---|---|---|---|---|
| | | | | | |
| | | | | | |
| | | | | | |
| | | | | | |

There is no accurate method of determining a direction in a moving vehicle. A magnetic vehicle-heading reference unit may be available in a few years, but for now use a compass. The navigator dismounts from the vehicle and moves away from the vehicle (at least 18 meters).

He sets the azimuth on the compass and picks a steering mark (rock, tree, hilltop) in the direction on that azimuth (See figure below).

NAVIGATING IN A VEHICLE

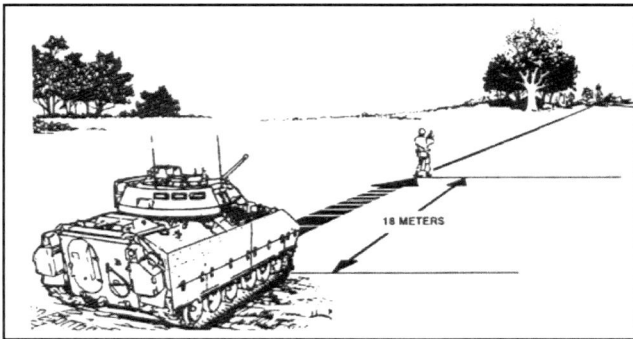

18 METERS

NAVIGATE

He remounts and has the driver identify the steering mark and proceeds to it in as straight a line as possible.

On arrival at the steering mark or on any changes in direction, he repeats the first three steps above for the next leg of travel.

**Without Steering Marks.** This procedure is used only on flat, featureless terrain.

The navigator dismounts from the vehicle, which is oriented in the direction of travel, and moves at least 18 meters to the front of the vehicle.

He faces the vehicle and reads the azimuth to the vehicle. By adding or subtracting 180º, he determines the forward azimuth (direction of travel).

On order from the navigator, the driver drives on a straight line to the navigator.

The navigator remounts the vehicle, holds the compass as it will be held while the vehicle is moving, and reads the azimuth in the direction of travel.

The compass will swing off the azimuth determined and pick up a constant deviation. For instance, say the azimuth was 75º while you were away from the vehicle. When you remounted and your driver drove straight forward, your compass showed 67º. You have a deviation of -8º. All you need to do is maintain that 67º compass heading to travel on a 75º magnetic heading.

At night, the same technique can be used. From the map, determine the azimuth you are to travel. Convert the grid azimuth to a magnetic azimuth. Line the vehicle up on that azimuth, then move well in front of it. Be sure it is aligned correctly. Then mount, have the driver move slowly forward, and note the deviation. If the vehicle has a turret, the above procedure works unless you traverse the turret; this changes the deviation.

The distance factor in dead reckoning is easy. Just determine the map distance to travel and add 20 percent to convert to ground distance. Use your vehicle odometer to be sure you travel the proper distance.

Another method, if you have a vehicle with a **stabilized turret,** is to align the turret on the azimuth you wish to travel, then switch the turret stabilization system on. The gun tube remains pointed at your destination no matter which way you turn the vehicle. This technique has been proven; it works. It is not harmful to the stabilization system. It is subject to stabilization drift, so use it for no more than 5,000 meters before resetting.

**NOTE:** If you have to take the turret off-line to engage a target, you will have to start all over, re-do the entire process.

Just like dismounted, it is best to use a combination of terrain association and dead reckoning. Terrain association is fast, is error-tolerant, and is best under most circumstances. It can be used day or night if you are proficient in it.

NAVIGATE

Dead reckoning is very accurate if you do everything correctly. You must be very precise. It is also slow, but it works on very flat terrain. You may use dead reckoning to travel across a large, flat area to a ridge, then use terrain association for the rest of the move. You must be able to use both methods. You should remember that your probable errors, in order of frequency, will be:

-Failure to determine distance to be traveled
-Failure to travel the proper distance
-Failure to properly plot or locate the objective
-Failure to select easily recognized checkpoints
-Failure to recognize speed of travel

## Desert

About 5 percent of the earth's land surface is covered by deserts. Deserts are large arid areas with little or no rainfall during the year. There are three types of deserts—mountain, rocky plateau, and sandy or dune deserts. All types of forces can be deployed in the desert. Armor and mechanized infantry forces are especially suitable to desert combat except in rough mountainous terrain where light infantry may be required. Airborne, air assault, and motorized forces can also be advanta- geously employed to exploit the vast distances charac- teristic of desert warfare.

In desert regions, terrain varies from nearly flat to lava beds and salt marshes. Mountain deserts contain scattered ranges or areas of barren hills or mountains.

NAVIGATE

The table below lists some of the world's major desert regions and their locations.

### Major Desert Locations

| REGION | LOCATION |
|---|---|
| Sahara | North Africa |
| Kalahari | Southwest Africa |
| Arabian | Southwest Asia |
| Gobi | Mongolia and Northern China |
| Rub'al Khali | South Arabia |
| Great Basin, Colorado, Chihuahua, Yuma Sonoran, and Mohave | Northern Mexico and Western United States |
| Takla Makan | Northern China |
| Kyzyl Kum | Southwest USSR |
| Kara Kum | Southwest USSR |
| Syrian | Saudi Arabia, Jordan, and Iraq |
| Great Victoria | Western and South Australia |
| Great Sandy | Northwestern Australia |
| Patagonia | Southern Argentina and Chile |
| Atacama | Northern Chile |

Finding the way in a desert presents some degree of difficulty for a person who has never been exposed to this environment. Desert navigators have learned their way through generations of experience.

Normally, desert people are nomadic, constantly moving in caravans. Navigating becomes second nature to them. Temperature in the tropical deserts reaches an average of 110° to 115° during the day, so most navigation takes place at night using the stars. Most deserts have some prevailing winds during the seasons. Such winds arrange the sand dunes in a specific pattern that gives the navigator the opportunity to determine the four cardinal directions. He may also use the sun's shadow-tip method.

A sense of direction can be obtained by watching desert animals on their way to and from water holes (oases). Water, navigation, and survival are closely related in desert areas. Most deserts have pigeons or doves, and their drinking habits are important to the navigator. As a rule, these birds never drink in the morning or during the day, making their evening flights the most important. When returning from the oases, their bodies are heavier from drinking and their flight is accompanied by a louder flapping of their wings.

Visibility is also an important factor in the desert, especially in judging distance. The absence of trees or other features prevents comparison between the horizon and the skyline.

Many desert maps are inaccurate, which makes up-to-date air, aerial photo, and ground reconnaissance necessary. In desert mountain areas contour intervals are generally large, so many of the intermediate relief features are not shown.

The desert normally permits observation and fire to maximum ranges. The terrain is generally wide open and the exceptionally clear atmosphere offers excellent long-range visibility. Combine this with a powerful sun and low cloud density and you have nearly unlimited light and visual clarity, which often contribute to gross underestimations of ranges. Errors of up to 200 or 300 percent are not uncommon. However, visibility conditions may be severely affected by sandstorms and mirages (heat shimmer caused by air rising from the extremely hot daytime desert surface), especially if the observer is looking into the sun through magnifying optical instruments.

When operating in the broad basins between mountain ranges or on rocky plateau deserts, there are frequently many terrain features to guide your movement by. But, observing these known features over great distances may provide a false sense of security in determining your precise location unless you frequently confirm your location by resection or referencing close-in terrain features. It is not uncommon to develop errors of several kilometers when casually estimating a position in this manner. Obviously, this can create many problems when attempting to locate a small checkpoint or objective, calling for CAS, reporting operational or intelligence information, or meeting CSS requirements.

When operating in an area with few visual cues, such as in a sandy or dune desert, or restricted visibility by a sandstorm or darkness, you must proceed by dead reckoning. The four steps and two techniques for navigation presented earlier remain valid in the desert. However, understanding the special conditions found there are extremely helpful as you apply them.

NAVIGATE

Tactical mobility and speed are key to successful desert operations. Obstacles and areas such as lava beds or salt marshes, which preclude surface movements, do exist. But most deserts permit two dimensional movement by ground forces similar to that of a naval task force at sea. Speed of execution is essential. Everyone moves farther and faster on the desert. Special navigation aids sometimes used in the desert include:

**Sun compass.** It can be used on moving vehicles and sextants. It requires accurate timekeeping. However, the deviation on a magnetic compass that is caused by the metal and electronics in the vehicle is usually less than +10°.

**Gyro compass.** The gun azimuth stabilizer is in fact a gyro compass. If used on fairly flat ground, it is useful for maintaining direction over limited distances.

**Fires.** Planned tracer fire or mortar and artillery concentrations (preferably smoke during the day and illumination at night) provide useful checks on estimated locations.

**Prepositioned lights.** This method consists of placing two or more searchlights far apart, behind the line of contact, beyond enemy artillery range, and concealed from enemy ground observation. Units in the area can determine their own locations through resection, using the vertical beams of the lights. These lights must be moved on a time schedule known to all friendly units.

One final note on desert navigation is that the sand, hard-baked ground, rocky surfaces, thorny vegetation, and heat generally found in the desert impose far greater demands for maintenance than you would plan for in temperate regions. It may also take longer to perform that maintenance. You also must be mounted. You cannot survive more than several days in the desert dismounted.

## MOUNTAIN TERRAIN

Mountains are generally understood to be larger than hills. Rarely do mountains occur individually; in most cases, they are found in elongated ranges or circular groups. When they are linked together, they constitute a mountain system. Light forces (infantry, airborne, special operations, and air assault forces) can operate effectively in mountainous regions because they are not terrain limited. Heavy forces must operate in passes and valleys that are negotiable by vehicle. The major mountain systems are listed in the table below.

NAVIGATE

### MAJOR MOUNTAIN LOCATIONS

| SYSTEM | LOCATION |
|---|---|
| The Andes | Central and South America |
| The Rockies | North America (USA-Canada) |
| The Appalachians | North America (USA-Canada) |
| The Alps | Central Europe |
| The Himalayas | Asia |
| The Caucasus | Western Asia and Europe (Russia) |

Because of the elevations, it is always colder (3° to 5° per 300-meter gain in altitude) and wetter than you might expect. Wind speeds can increase the effects of the cold even more. Sudden severe storms and fog are encountered regularly. Below the tree line, vegetation is heavy because of the extra rainfall and the fact that the land is rarely cleared for farming.

The heights of mountainous terrain permit excellent long-range observation. However, rapidly fluctuating weather with frequent periods of high winds, rain, snow, or fog may limit visibility. Also, the rugged nature of the terrain frequently produces significant dead space at mid-ranges.

Reduced mobility, compartmented terrain, and the effects of rapidly changing weather increase the importance of air, ground, aerial photo, and map recon-naissance. Since mountain maps often use large contour intevals, microrelief interpretation and detailed terrain analysis require special emphasis.

At first glance, some mountainous terrain may not appear to offer adequate cover and concealment; however, you can improve the situation. When moving, use rock outcroppings, boulders, and heavy vegetation for cover and concealment; use terrain features to mask maneuvers. Use harsh weather, which often obscures observation, to enhance concealment.

NAVIGATE

Since there are only a few routing options, all-around
security must be of primary concern. Natural obstacles
are everywhere, and the enemy can easily construct
more. You must constantly be prepared for ambushes.

Existing roads and trails offer the best routes for
movement. Off-road movement may enhance security
provided there is detailed reconnaissance, photo intelligence, or information from local inhabitants to ensure
the route is negotiable. Again, the four steps and two
techniques for navigation presented earlier remain valid
in the mountains. Nevertheless, understanding the special
conditions and the terrain will help you navigate. Other
techniques that are sometimes helpful in mountains are:

**Aspect of Slope.** To determine the aspect of slope, take
a compass reading along an imaginary line that runs
straight down the slope. It should cut through each of
the contour lines at about a 90° angle. By checking the
map and knowing the direction of slope where you are
located, you will be able to keep track of your location,
and it will help guide your cross-country movement
even when visibility is poor.

**Use of an Altimeter.** Employment of an altimeter with
calibrations on the scale down to 10 or 20 meters
is helpful to land navigators moving in areas where
radical changes in elevation exist. An altimeter is a
type of barometer that gauges air pressure, except
it measures on an adjustable scale marked in feet or

NAVIGATE

meters of elevation rather than in inches or centime-
ters of mercury. Careful use of the altimeter helps to
pinpoint your position on a map through a unique type
of resection. Instead of finding your position by using
two different directional values, you use one directional
value and one elevation value.

A final note on navigation in the mountains is that there
are ample terrain features, but be careful not to confuse
what mountain for another especially when calling in CAS.
Also, many Soldiers get blisters on the sides of their feet
from walking on the sides of mountains.

### Jungle Terrain

These large geographic regions are found within the
tropics near the equator (Central America, along the
Amazon River, South-Eastern Asia and adjacent islands,
and vast areas in the middle of Africa and India). Jungles
are characterized as rainy, humid areas with heavy
layers of tangled, impenetrable vegetation. Jungles
contain many species of wildlife (tigers, monkeys,
parrots, snakes, alligators, and so forth). The jungle is
also a paradise for insects, which are the worst enemy
of the navigator because some insects carry diseases
(malaria, yellow fever, cholera, and so forth). While
navigating in these areas, very little terrain association
can be accomplished because of the heavy foliage. Dead
reckoning is one of the methods used in these areas. A
lost navigator in the jungle can eventually find his way

NAVIGATE

back to civilization by following any body of water with a downstream flow. However, not every civilization found is of a friendly nature.

Operations in jungles tend to be isolated actions by small forces because of the difficulties encountered in moving and in maintaining contact between units. Divisions can move cross-country slowly; but, aggressive reconnaissance, meticulous intelligence collection, and detailed coordination are required to concentrate forces in this way. More commonly, large forces operate along roads or natural avenues of movement, as was the case in the mountains. Patrolling and other surveillance operations are especially important to ensure security of larger forces in the close terrain of jungles.

Short fields of observation and fire, and thick vegetation make maintaining contact with the enemy difficult. The same factors reduce the effectiveness of indirect fire and make jungle combat primarily a fight between infantry forces. Support by air and mechanized forces can be decisive at times, but it will not always be available or effective.

Jungles are characterized by high temperatures, heavy rains, high humidity, and an abundance of vegetation. The climate varies with location. Close to the equator, all seasons are nearly alike with heavy rains all year. Farther from the equator (India and Southeast Asia), there are distinct wet (monsoon) and dry seasons.

NAVIGATE

Both zones have high temperatures (averaging 75 to 95+ degrees Fahrenheit), heavy rainfall (as much as 400+ inches annually, and high humidity, 90 percent) all year.

In temperate climates, it is the areas of vegetation that are most likely to be altered and incorrectly portrayed on a map. In jungle areas, the vegetation grows so rapidly that it is more likely to be cleared and make these areas be shown incorrectly.

The jungle environment includes dense forests, grasslands, swamps, and cultivated areas. Forests are classified as primary and secondary based upon the terrain and vegetation. Primary forests include tropical rain forests and deciduous forests. Secondary forests are found at the edges of both rain forests and deciduous forests and in areas where jungles have been cleared and abandoned. These places are typically overgrown with weeds, grasses, thorns, ferns, canes, and shrubs. Movement is especially slow and difficult. The extremely thick vegetation reaches a height of 2 meters and severely limits observation to only a few meters.

Tropical rain forests consist mostly of large trees whose branches spread and lock together to form canopies. These canopies, which can exist at two and three different levels, may form as low as 10 meters from the ground. They prevent direct sunlight from reaching the ground, causing a lack of undergrowth on the jungle floor.

NAVIGATE

Extensive above-ground root systems and hanging vines are common and make vehicular travel difficult; foot movement is easier. Ground observation is limited to about 50 meters and air observation is nearly impossible.

Deciduous forests are in semitropical zones that have both wet and dry seasons. In the wet season, trees are fully leaved; in the dry season, much of the foliage dies. Trees are usually less dense than in rain forests, which allows more sunlight to filter to the ground. This procedure produces thick undergrowth. During the wet season, air and ground observation is limited and movement is difficult. During the dry season, both improve.

Swamps are common to all low, jungle areas where there is poor drainage. When navigating in a swampy area, a careful analysis of map and ground should be taken before any movement. The soldiers should travel in small numbers with only the equipment required for their mission, keeping in mind that they are going to be immersed in water part of the time. The usual technique used in swamp navigation is dead reckoning. There are two basic types of swamps—mangrove and palm. Mangrove swamps are found in coastal areas wherever tides influence water flow. Mangrove is a shrub-like tree that grows 1 to 5 meters high. These trees have a tangled root system, both above and below the waterline, which restricts movement either by foot or small boat. Observation on the ground and from the air is poor, but concealment is excellent.

NAVIGATE

Grassy plains or savannas are generally located away from the equator but within the tropics. These vast land areas are characterized by flatlands with a different type of vegetation than jungles. They consist mainly of grasses (ranging from 1 to more than 12 feet in height), shrubs, and isolated trees. The most difficult areas to navigate are the ones surrounded by tall grass (elephant grass); however, vehicles can negotiate here better than in some areas. There are few or no natural features to navigate by, making dead reckoning or navigation by stars the only technique for movement. Depending on the height of the grass, ground observation may vary from poor to good. Concealment from air observation is poor for both soldiers and vehicles.

Bamboo stands are common throughout the tropics. They should be bypassed whenever possible. They are formidable obstacles for vehicles, and soldier movement through them is slow, exhausting, and noisy.

Cultivated areas exist in jungles also. They range from large, well-planned, well-managed farms and plantations to small tracts, cultivated by farmers. The three general types of cultivated areas are rice paddies, plantations, and small farms.

Areas such as jungles are generally not accurately mapped because heavy vegetation makes aerial surveys difficult. The ability to observe terrain features, near or far, is extremely limited. The navigator must rely heavily upon

NAVIGATE

his compass and the dead reckoning technique when moving in the jungle. Navigation is further complicated by the inability to make straight-line movements. Terrain analysis, constant use of the compass, and an accurate pace count are essential to navigation in this environment.

Rates of movement and pace counts are particularly important to jungle navigators. The most common error is to overestimate the distance traveled. The distances in the table below can be used as a rough guide for the maximum distances that might be traveled in various types of terrain during one hour in daylight.

EST. DISTANCE BY TERRAIN PER HOUR

| Type of Terrain | Maximum Distance (In Meters) |
|---|---|
| Tropical rain forest | up to 1,000 |
| Deciduous forest | 500 |
| Secondary jungle | 100 to 500 |
| Tall grass | 500 |
| Swamps | 100 to 300 |
| Rice paddies (wet) | 800 |
| Rice paddies (dry) | 2,000 |
| Plantations | 2,000 |
| Trails | up to 3,000 |

NAVIGATE

Special navigation strategies that are helpful
in jungles include:

**Personal pace table.** You should either make a mental
or written personal pace table that includes your average
pace count per 100 meters for each of the types of terrain
through which you are likely to navigate.

**Resection using indirect fire.** Call for mortar or
artillery fire (airbursts of white phosphorous or illumination) on two widely separated grids that are not on
terrain features like the one you are occupying and are a
safe distance from your estimated location. Directions to
the airbursts sometimes must be determined by sound.

**Modified area/point navigation.** Even when making
primary use of the compass for dead reckoning, you
are frequently able to area navigate to an expanded
objective, which is easily identified by terrain association. Then, simply develop a short, point-navigation leg
to your final destination.

## ARCTIC

Arctic terrain includes those areas that experience
extended periods of below freezing temperatures. In
these areas, the ground is generally covered with ice or
snow during the winter season. Although frozen ground
and ice can improve trafficability, a deep accumulation of
snow can reduce it. Vehicles and personnel require special
equipment and care under these adverse conditions.

Both the terrain and the type and size of unit operations
vary greatly in arctic areas. In open terrain, armored and
mechanized forces will be effective although they will
have to plan and train for the special conditions. In broken
terrain, forests, and mountains, light forces will predomi-
nate as usual. However, foot movement can take up to five
times as long as it might under warmer conditions.

Both the terrain and cultural features you may confront
in winter may vary to any extreme, as can the weather.
The common factor is an extended period of below-
freezing temperatures. The terrain may be plains,
plateaus, hills, or mountains. The climate will be cold,
but the weather will vary greatly from place to place.
Most arctic terrain experiences snow, but some claim
impressive accumulations each season, such as the
lake-effected snow belts off Lake Ontario near Fort
Drum, New York. Other areas have many cold days with
sunshine and clear nights, and little snow accumulation.

In areas with distinct local relief and scattered trees or
forests, the absence of foliage makes movement by terrain
association easier; observation and fields of fire are greatly
enhanced except during snowstorms. But in relatively
flat, open areas covered with snow (especially in bright
sunlight), the resulting lack of contrast may interfere
with your being able to read the land. With foliage gone,
concealment (both from the ground and from the air) is
greatly reduced. As in desert areas, you must make better
use of the terrain to conceal your movements.

NAVIGATE

Frozen streams and swamps may no longer be obstacles, and thus identification of avenues of approach may be difficult in winter. However, the concept as to what is key terrain is not likely to be affected.

Special skills may be required in arctic terrain, such as the proper use of winter clothing, skis, and snowshoes; but this does not affect your navigation strategies. There are no special techniques for navigating in arctic terrain. Just be aware of the advantages and disadvantages that may present themselves and make the most of your opportunities while applying the four steps and two techniques for land navigation.

Remember, the highest caliber of leadership is required to ensure that all necessary tasks are performed, that security is maintained, and that soldiers and their equipment are protected from the physical effects of very low temperatures. There is a great temptation to do less than a thorough job at whatever the task may be when you are very cold.

Night navigation may be particularly enhanced when operating in arctic terrain. Moonlight and starlight on a clear night reflect off the snow, thus enabling you to employ daytime terrain association techniques with little difficulty. Even cloudy winter nights are often brighter than clear moonlit summer nights when the ground is dark and covered with foliage. Movements with complete light discipline (no black-out drives)

NAVIGATE

can often be executed. On the other hand, areas with severe winter climates experience lengthy periods of darkness each day, which may be accompanied by driving snow and limited visibility.

## Urban Areas

The world continues to become more urbanized each year; therefore, it is unlikely that all fighting will be done in rural settings. Major urban areas represent the power and wealth of a particular country in the form of industrial bases, transportation complexes, economic institutions, and political and cultural centers. Therefore, it may be necessary to secure and neutralize them. When navigating in urban places, it is man-made features, such as roads, railroads, bridges, and buildings that become important, while terrain and vegetation become less useful.

Military operations on urbanized terrain require detailed planning that provides for decentralized execution. As a result of the rapid growth and changes occurring in many urban areas, the military topographic map is likely to be outdated. Supplemental use of commercially produced city maps may be helpful, or an up-to-date sketch can be made.

Urbanized terrain normally offers many AAs for mounted maneuver well forward of and leading to urban centers. In the proximity of these built-up areas, however, such approach routes generally become choked by urban sprawl and perhaps by the nature of adjacent

NAVIGATE

natural terrain. Dismounted forces then make the most of available cover by moving through buildings and underground systems, along edges of streets, and over rooftops. Urban areas tend to separate and isolate units, requiring the small-unit leader to take the initiative and demonstrate his skill in order to prevail.

The urban condition of an area creates many obstacles, and the destruction of many buildings and bridges as combat power is applied during a battle further limits your freedom of movement. Cover and concealment are plentiful, but observation and fields of fire are greatly restricted.

Navigation in urban areas can be confusing, but there are often many cues that will present themselves as you proceed. They include streets and street signs; building styles and sizes; the urban geography of industrial, warehousing, residential housing, and market districts; man-made transportation features other than streets and roads (rail and trolley lines); and the terrain features and hydrographic features located within the built-up area. Strategies for staying on the route in an urban area include:

- Write down or memorize the route through an urban area as a step-by-step process. For example, "Go three blocks north, turn left (west) on a wide divided boulevard until you go over a river bridge. Turn right (north) along the west bank of the river, and. . ."

- While studying the map and operating in a built-up area, work hard to develop an understanding (mental map) of the entire area. This advantage will allow you to navigate over multiple routes to any location. It will also preclude you getting lost whenever you miss a turn or are forced off the planned route by obstacles or the tactical situation.

- Whenever you have a vantage point to two or more known features portrayed on the map, do not hesitate to use either estimated or plotted resection to pinpoint your position. These opportunities are often plentiful in an urban setting.

FalconView and satellite images are common tools provided to Soldiers to navigate and find target buildings in urban environments.

## NAVIGATING AT NIGHT
*1 Click = 3 Degrees*
This is the absolute most important thing to remember about navigating at night. I will touch on this again at the end of this section.

The land nav test courses for Ranger School and SFAS begin in the dark and end during daylight. In order to pass these courses, you must be comfortable navigating at night. The basic technique used for nighttime land navigation is dead reckoning. At night you will take smaller steps so it is imperative that you have a separate pace count for night navigation. Also, at night people tend to walk in a clockwise circle if they don't stay on azimuth.

NAVIGATE

*1 Click = 3 Degrees. 1 click of the bezel ring is 3 degrees.*

To set your compass at night Rotate the bezel ring until the luminous line is over the fixed black index line.

Find the desired azimuth and divide it by three. The result is the number of clicks that you have to rotate the bezel ring.

Count the desired number of clicks. If the desired azimuth is smaller than 180°, the number of clicks on the bezel ring should be counted in a counterclockwise direction. For example, the desired azimuth is 51°. Desired azimuth is 51°, 3 = 17 clicks counterclockwise. If the desired azimuth is larger than 180°, subtract the number of degrees from 360° and divide by 3 to obtain the number of clicks. Count them in a clockwise direction. For example, the desired azimuth is 330°; 360° - 330° = 30, 3 = 10 clicks clockwise.

With the compass preset as described above, assume a centerhold technique and rotate your body until the north-seeking arrow is aligned with the luminous line on the bezel. Then proceed forward in the direction of the front cover's luminous dots, which are aligned with the fixed black index line containing the azimuth.

When the compass is to be used in darkness, an initial azimuth should be set while light is still available, if possible. With the initial azimuth as a base, any other azimuth that is a multiple of three can be established through the use of the clicking feature of the bezel ring.

NAVIGATE

**NOTE:** Sometimes the desired azimuth is not exactly divisible by three, causing an option of rounding up or rounding down. If the azimuth is rounded up, this causes an increase in the value of the azimuth, and the object is to be found on the left. If the azimuth is rounded down, this causes a decrease in the value of the azimuth, and the object is to be found on the right.

## Tactical Considerations

Military cross-country navigation is intellectually demanding because it is imperative that the unit, crew, or vehicle survive and successfully complete the move in order to accomplish its mission. However, the unnecessary use of a difficult route makes navigation too complicated, creates more noise when proceeding over it, causes wear and tear on equipment and personnel, increases the need for and needlessly complicate recovery operations, and wastes scarce time. On receipt of a tactical mission, the leader begins his troop-leading procedures and makes a tentative plan. He bases the tentative plan on a good terrain analysis. He analyzes the considerations covered in the following mnemonics (OCOKA and METT-T).

NAVIGATE

## OCOKA

O – Observation and Fields of Fire
C – Cover and Concealment
O - Obstacles
K – Key Terrain
A – Avenues of Approach

The terrain should be analyzed for observation and fields of fire, cover and concealment, obstacles, key terrain, and avenues of approach.

**Observation and Fields of Fire.** The purpose of observation is to see the enemy (or various landmarks) but not be seen by him. Anything that can be seen can be hit. Therefore, a field of fire is an area that a weapon or a group of weapons can cover effectively with fire from a given position.

**Cover and Concealment.** Cover is shelter or protection (from enemy fire) either natural or artificial. Always try to use covered routes and seek cover for each halt, no matter how brief it is planned to be.

Unfortunately, two factors interfere with obtaining constant cover. One is time and the other is terrain. Concealment is protection from observation or surveillance, including concealment from enemy air observation. Before, trees provided good concealment, but with modern thermal and infrared imaging equipment, trees are not always effective. When you are moving, concealment is

NAVIGATE

generally secondary; therefore, select routes and positions that do not allow covered or concealed enemy near you.

**Obstacles.** Obstacles are any obstructions that stop, delay, or divert movement. Obstacles can be natural (rivers, swamps, cliffs, or mountains) or they may be artificial (barbed wire entanglements, pits, concrete or metal antimechanized traps). They can be ready-made or constructed in the field. Always consider any possible obstacles along your movement route and, if possible, try to keep obstacles between the enemy and yourself.

**Key Terrain.** Key terrain is any locality or area that the seizure or retention of affords a marked advantage to either combatant. Urban areas that are often seen by higher headquarters as being key terrain because they are used to control routes. On the other hand, an urban area that is destroyed may be an obstacle instead. High ground can be key because it dominates an area with good observation and fields of fire. In an open area, a draw or wadi (dry streambed located in an arid area) may provide the only cover for many kilometers, thereby becoming key. You should always attempt to locate any area near you that could be even remotely considered as key terrain.

**Avenues of Approach.** These are access routes. They may be the routes you can use to get to the enemy or the routes they can use to get to you. Basically, an identifiable route that approaches a position or location is an avenue of approach to that location. They are often terrain corridors such as valleys or wide, open areas.

NAVIGATE

## METT-T

M - Mission
E - Enemy
T - Terrain
T - Troops
T - Time Available

Tactical factors other than the military aspects of terrain must also be considered in conjunction with terrain during movement planning and execution as well. These additional considerations are mission, enemy, terrain and weather, troops, and time available.

**Mission.** This refers to the specific task assigned to a unit or individual. It is the duty or task together with the purpose that clearly indicates the action to be taken and the reason for it—but not how to do it. Training exercises should stress the importance of a thorough map reconnaissance to evaluate the terrain. This allows the leader to confirm his tentative plan, basing his decision on the terrain's effect on his mission.

Marches by foot or vehicle are used to move troops from one location to another. Soldiers must get to the right place, at the right time, and in good fighting condition. The normal rate for an 8 hour foot march is 4 kmph.

However, the rate of march may vary, depending on the following factors:

    -Distance
    -Time Allowed
    -Likelihood of enemy contact
    -Terrain
    -Weather
    -Physical Condition of Soldiers
    -Weight to be carried

Patrol missions are used to conduct combat or reconnaissance operations. Without detailed planning and a thorough map reconnaissance, any patrol mission may not succeed. During the map reconnaissance, the mission leader determines a primary and alternate route to and from the objectives.

Movement to contact is conducted whenever an element is moving toward the enemy but is not in contact with the enemy. The lead element must orient its movement on the objective by conducting a map reconnaissance, determining the location of the objective on both the map and the ground, and selecting the route to be taken.

Delays and withdrawals are conducted to slow the enemy down without becoming decisively engaged, or to assume another mission. To be effective, the element leader must know where he is to move and the route to be taken.

NAVIGATE

**Enemy.** This refers to the strength, status of training, disposition (locations), doctrine, capabilities, equipment (including night vision devices), and probable courses of action that impact upon both the planning and execution of the mission, including a movement.

**Terrain and Weather.** Observation and fields of fire influence the placement of positions and crewserved weapons. The leader conducts a map reconnaissance to determine key terrain, obstacles, cover and concealment, and likely avenues of approach.

Key terrain is any area whose control affords a marked advantage to the force holding it. Some types of key terrain are high ground, bridges, towns, and road junctions.

Obstacles are natural or man-made terrain features that stop, slow down, or divert movement. Consideration of obstacles is influenced by the unit's mission. An obstacle may be an advantage or disadvantage, depending upon the direction of attack or defense. Obstacles can be found by conducting a thorough map reconnaissance and study of recent aerial photographs.

Cover and concealment are determined for both friendly and enemy forces. Concealment is protection from observation; cover is protection from the effects of fire. Most terrain features that offer cover also provide concealment from ground observation. There are areas that provide no concealment from enemy observation. These danger areas may be large or small open fields, roads, or streams. During

NAVIGATE

the leader's map reconnaissance, he determines any obvious danger areas and, if possible, adjusts his route.

Avenues of approach are routes by which a unit may reach an objective or key terrain. To be considered an AA, a route must provide enough width for the deployment of the size force for which it is being considered. The AAs are also considered for the subordinate enemy force. For example, a company determines likely AAs for an enemy platoon; a platoon determines likely AAs for an enemy squad. Likely AAs may be either ridges, valleys, or by air. By examining the terrain, the leader determines the likely enemy AAs based on the tactical situation.

Weather has little effect on dismounted land navigation. Rain and snow could possibly slow down the rate of march, that is all. Heat could force more stops on the movement. But during mounted land navigation, the navigator must know the effect of weather on his vehicle.

**Troops.** Consideration of your own troops is equally important. The size and type of the unit to be moved and its capabilities, physical condition, status of training, and types of equipment assigned all affect the selection of routes, positions, fire plans, and the various decisions to be made during movement. On ideal terrain such as relatively level ground with little or no woods, a platoon can defend a front of up to 400 meters. The leader must conduct a thorough map reconnaissance and terrain analysis of the area his unit is to defend. Heavily wooded

NAVIGATE

areas or very hilly areas may reduce the front a platoon can defend. The size of the unit must also be taken into consideration when planning a movement to contact. During movement, the unit must retain its ability to maneuver. A small draw or stream may reduce the unit's maneuverability but provide excellent concealment. All of these factors must be considered.

Types of equipment that may be needed by the unit can be determined by a map reconnaissance. For example, if the unit must cross a large stream during its movement to the objective, ropes may be needed for safety lines.

Physical capabilities of the soldiers must be considered when selecting a route. Crossing a large swampy area may present no problem to a physically fit unit, but to a unit that has not been physically conditioned, the swampy area may slow or completely stop its movement.

**Time Available.** At times, the unit may have little time to reach an objective or to move from one point to another. The leader must conduct a map reconnaissance to determine the quickest route to the objective; this is not always a straight route. From point A to point B on the map may appear to be 1,000 meters, but if the route is across a large ridge, the distance will be greater. Another route from point A to B may be 1,500 meters—but on flat terrain. In this case, the quickest route would be across the flat terrain; however, concealment and cover may be lost.

One key to success in tactical missions is the ability to move undetected to the objective. There are four steps to land navigation. Being given an objective and the requirement to move there, you must know where you are, plan the route, stay on the route, and recognize the objective.

Three route-selection criteria that are important for small-unit movements are cover, concealment, and the availability of reliable checkpoint features. The latter is weighted even more heavily when selecting the route for a night operation. The degree of visibility and ease of recognition (visual effect) are the key to the proper selection of these features.

**The best checkpoints are linear features that cross the route.** Examples include perennial streams, hard-top roads, ridges, valleys, railroads, and power transmission lines. Next, it is best to select features that represent elevation changes of at least two contour intervals such as hills, depressions, spurs, and draws. Primary reliance upon cultural features and vegetation is cautioned against because they are most likely to have changed since the map was last revised.

Checkpoints located at places where changes in direction are made mark your **decision points.** Be especially alert to see and recognize these features during movement. During preparation and planning, it is especially important to review the route and anticipate where mistakes are most likely to be made so they can be avoided.

NAVIGATE

Following a valley floor or proceeding near (not on) the crest of a ridgeline generally offers easy movement, good navigation checkpoints, and sufficient cover and concealment. It is best to follow terrain features whenever you can—not to fight them.

A lost or a late arriving unit, or a tired unit that is tasked with an unnecessarily difficult move, does not contribute to the accomplishment of a mission. On the other hand, the unit that moves too quickly and carelessly into a destructive ambush or leaves itself open to air strikes also have little effect. Careful planning and study are required each time a movement route is to be selected.

## TACTICAL STRIP MAP

Since only key leaders have maps, a good technique for tactical movements is to draw strip maps on luminous tape and give one to each Soldier. Put acetate over the luminous tape and you can use a grease pencil and draw the terrain features from the map so the Soldiers can keep up with the movement and see it at night.

Before departing on tactical missions ensure all maps and overlays are sterilized. If you must have points marked on the map, just have the dots on the map, but nothing labeling what they are and all overlays should be destroyed. You don't want to risk these falling into enemy hands.

NAVIGATE

# CHAPTER 8:
# FIELD EXPEDIENT
# METHODS FOR DIRECTION

## SHADOW TIP METHOD

The shadow tip method is a simple way to determine direction by following the 4 steps below.

Step 1. Place a stick or branch into the ground at a level spot where a distinctive shadow will be cast. Mark the shadow tip with a stone, twig, or other means. This first shadow mark is always the west direction.

Step 2. Wait 10 to 15 minutes until the shadow tip moves a few inches. Mark the new position of the shadow tip in the same way as the first.

Step 3. Draw a straight line through the two marks to obtain an approximate east-west line.

Step 4. Standing with the first mark (west) to your left, the other directions are simple; north is to the front, east is to the right, and south is behind you.

A line drawn perpendicular to the east-west line at any point is the approximate north-south line. If you are uncertain which direction is east and which is west, observe this simple rule--the first shadow-tip mark is always in the west direction, everywhere on earth.

## SHADOW TIP METHOD

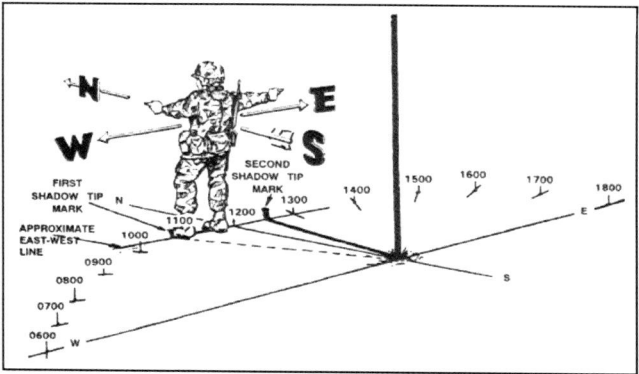

## THE WATCH METHOD

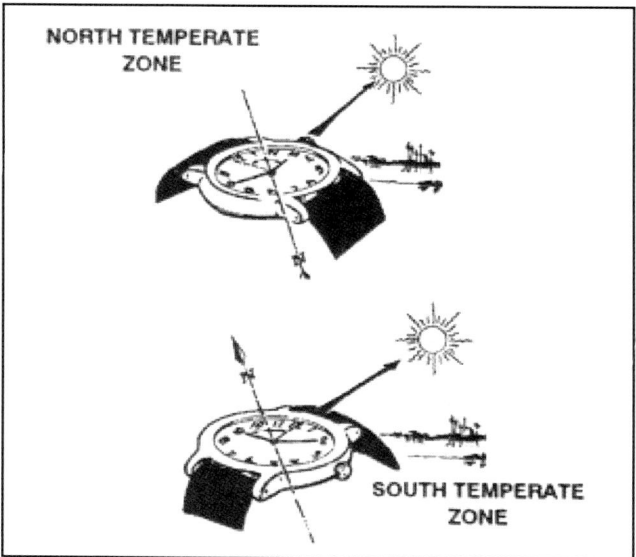

## THE WATCH METHOD

A watch can be used to determine the approximate true north and true south. In the north temperate zone only, the hour hand is pointed toward the sun. A south line can be found midway between the hour hand and 1200 hours, standard time. If on daylight saving time, the north-south line is found between the hour hand and 1300 hours. If there is any doubt as to which end of the line is north, remember that the sun is in the east before noon and in the west after noon.

The watch may also be used to determine direction in the south temperate zone; however, the method is different. The 1200-hour dial is pointed toward the sun, and halfway between 1200 hours and the hour hand will be a north line. If on daylight saving time, the north line lies midway between the hour hand and 1300 hours.

## The Star Method

Less than 60 of approximately 5,000 stars visible to the eye are used by navigators. The stars seen as we look up at the sky at night are not evenly scattered across the whole sky. Instead they are in groups called constellations.

The constellations that we see depends partly on where we are located on the earth, the time of the year, and the time of the night. The night changes with the seasons because of the journey of the earth around the sun, and it also changes from hour to hour because the turning of the earth makes some constellations seem to travel in a circle. But there is one star that is in almost exactly the same place in the sky all night long every night. It is the North Star, also known as the Polar Star or Polaris.

The North Star is less than 1° off true north and does not move from its place because the axis of the earth is pointed toward it. The North Star is in the group of stars called the Little Dipper. It is the last star in the handle of the dipper. There are two stars in the Big Dipper, which are a big help when trying to find the North Star. They are called the Pointers, and an imaginary line drawn through them five times their distance points to the North Star. There are many stars brighter than the North Star, but none is more important because of its location. However, the North Star can only be seen in the northern hemisphere so it cannot serve as a guide south of the equator. The farther one goes north, the higher the North Star is in the sky, and above latitude 70°, it is too high in the sky to be useful.

## THE STAR METHOD

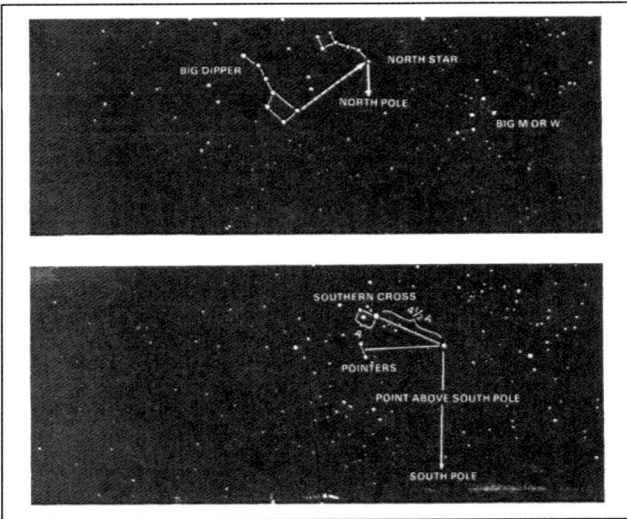

Depending on the star selected for navigation, azimuth checks are necessary. A star near the north horizon serves for about half an hour. When moving south, azimuth checks should be made every 15 minutes. When traveling east or west, the difficulty of staying on azimuth is caused more by the likelihood of the star climbing too high in the sky or losing itself behind the western horizon than it is by the star changing direction angle. When this happens, it is necessary to change to another guide star. The Southern Cross is the main constellation used as a guide south of the equator, and the above general directions for using north and south stars are reversed. When navigating using the stars as guides, the user must know the different constellation shapes and their locations throughout the world.

# Constellations in the Northern Hemisphere

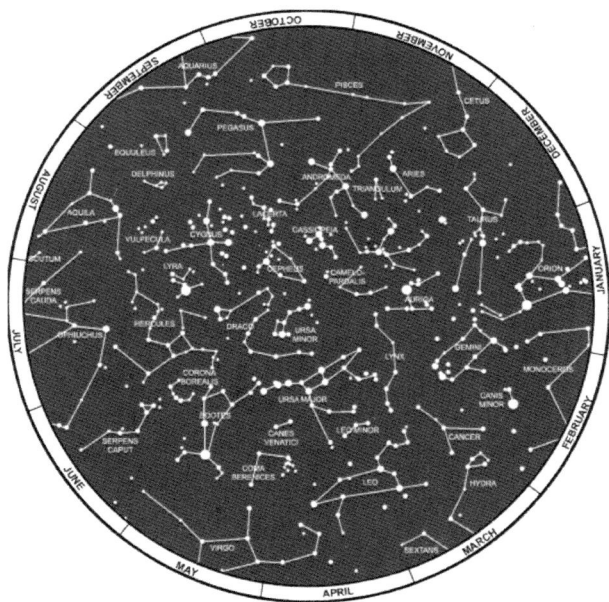

# Constellations in the Southern Hemisphere

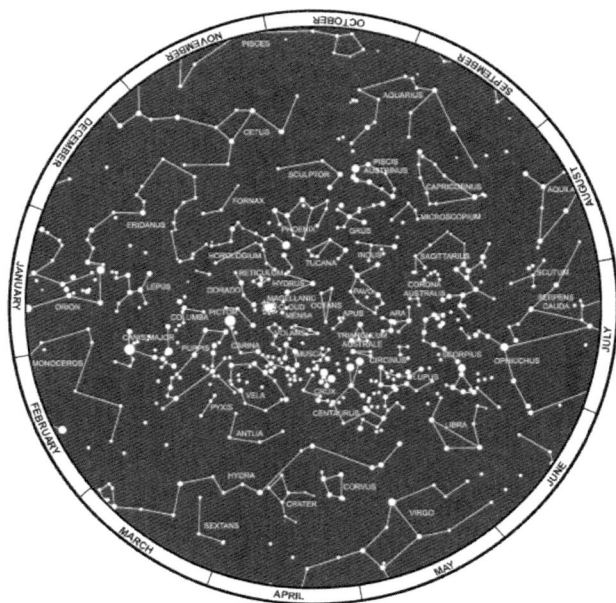

## Improvised Compass

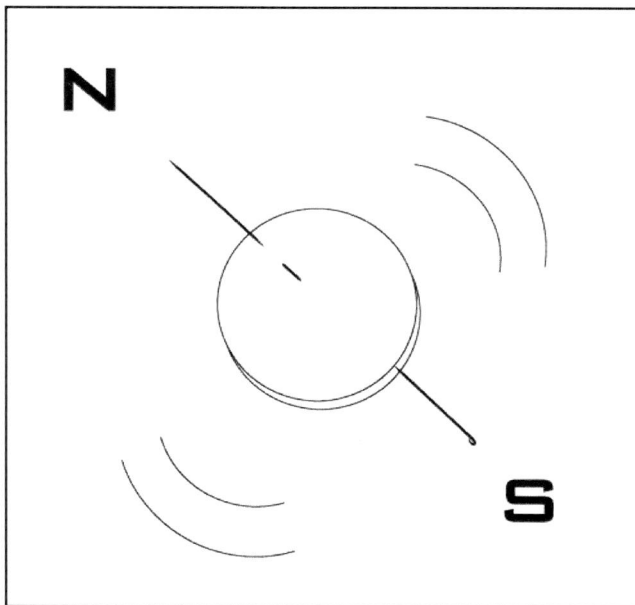

## Improvised Compass

If you don't have a compass, you can create your own in much the same way people did hundreds of years ago. To create your own compass, you will need the following materials:

A needle or some other wire-like piece of steel (a straightened paper clip, for example)

Something small that floats such as a piece of cork, the bottom of a Styrofoam coffee cup, a piece of plastic or the cap from a milk jug

A dish, preferably a pie plate, 9 to 12 inches in diameter, with about an inch of water in it

The first step is to turn the needle into a magnet. The easiest way to do this is with another magnet -- stroke the magnet along the needle 10 or 20 times. If you are having trouble finding a magnet, two possible sources include a can opener or the magnet from inside your cellphone (usually part of the speaker).

Place your float in the middle of the dish of water. Place your needle on the center of the float and it will slowly point toward magnetic north.

## Moss

There have been many articles written and survival experts claim that you can tell cardinal direction by the side of a tree that moss grows on. The premise is that moss only grows on the North side of trees to shun sunlight. **This is simply not true.** Moss will grow wherever it can find moisture. If the south side of a tree you are looking at is partly shaded by another tree, then moss will colonize it. It may be that in certain places and under certain conditions that moss grows predominantly on the north side of trees, but not enough to recommend relying on the moss to find your way.

# NOTES:

# CHAPTER 9:
# MAP FOLDING

Figures B-1 and B-2 show ways of folding maps to make them small enough to be carried easily and still be available for use without having to unfold them entirely.

The key is to have your land nav course, or area of operations the only visible area. I like to use binder clips to hold the map in place after I have folded it. On land nav courses, when my map isn't in my hand I keep it in my cargo pocket so it is easily accessible. Others like to tuck their map into the top of their shirt. I recommend tying down your map or the baggie it is in so you don't lose it.

## TWO METHODS OF FOLDING A MAP

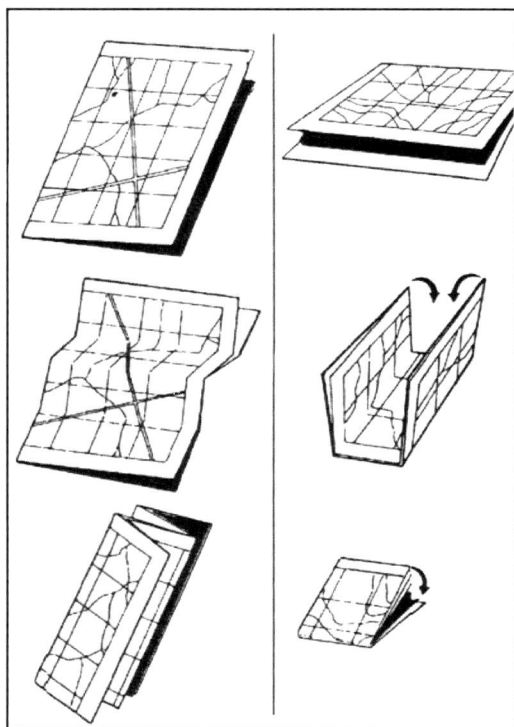

## How to slit and fold a map for special use

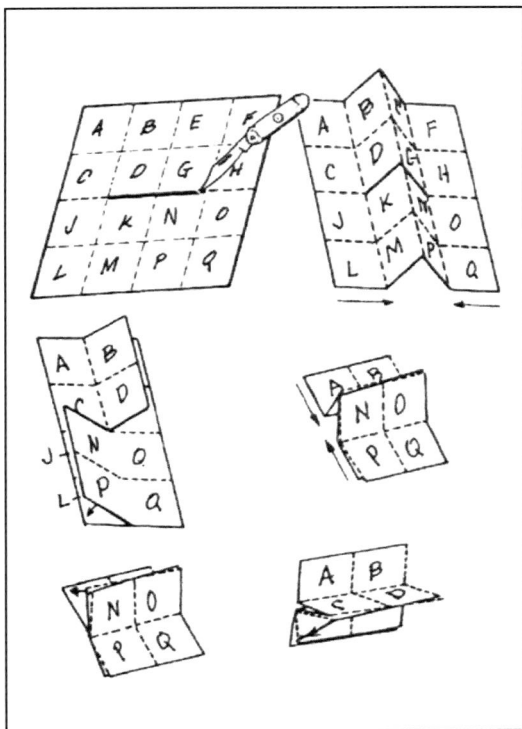

## NOTES:

# CHAPTER 10:
# TIPS & TRICKS

## PACE COUNT

The average Soldier uses 116 paces to travel 100 meters. Check your pace length by practicing on a known 100-meter distance, like a football field plus one end zone, which totals 110 yards (about 100 meters).

When you travel cross-country as you do in the field, you use more paces to travel 100 meters, usually about 148 instead of 116. This is because you are traveling over uneven ground and must use more paces to make up for your movement up and down hills.

You should check your pace over at least 600 meters of crisscrossing terrain to learn how many paces it takes you to travel an average 100 meters over such terrain.

Be sure you know how many paces it takes you to walk 100 meters on both level and crisscrossing terrain.

For keeping track of your distance travelled you can put 10 pebbles in your right pocket. When you go 100 meters, move one pebble to your left pocket and start your count over. When all 10 pebbles have been moved to your left pocket, you have traveled 1 kilometer. You can use this technique if you don't have ranger beads or 550 cord with slidable knots.

## COMPENSATING FOR DRIFT

Because people tend to drift even when trying to walk a straight line, a good technique is to alternate which side of a tree you walk around. For example, the first tree you come to walk around the left side of it. The next tree you encounter, walk around the right side of it. This prevents left handed people from drifting to the left and right handed people from drifting to the right.

If you always hold your compass in your right hand and are right handed always go around every tree on the left side and vice versa.

Always double check all of your plots before departing on a land nav course. Like a carpenter, measure twice, cut once!

## SHOOTING THE AZIMUTH

During daylight, once you are facing the azimuth you wish to travel on, line up the luminous line on the compass with the north seeking narrow. Using the centerhold method, all you have to do when you walk is ensure the north seeking arrow stays aligned with the luminous line and you are staying on azimuth.

Another trick is to shoot your azimuth with the cheek to compass method to a specific tree or object and then put your compass away and walk to that object. Once there, repeat the process staying on azimuth.

## ORIENTEERING CLUB

Join an orienteering club in your area. Do a google search to find one nearest you. This will greatly improve your land nav skills.

## COMPASS STORAGE

To easily access your compass, loop the metal ring over a chest pocket button and it will hang from your shirt for easy access so you don't have to keep taking it out of the pouch.

Use the lanyard on the compass to tie it down to your gear or through a button hole.

Always carry a second lensatic compass with you in the event yours gets broken, lost, etc.

## NAVIGATION TECHNIQUES

**Try to parallel roads as much as possible.**

Navigate to an intersection near your point and then use them as attack points to be able to dead reckon to your point.

Identify backstops so you know if you have gone too far and missed your point.

Identify and keep up with checkpoints along your route. This will prevent your mind from drifting while you walk. It is important to stay concentrated and alert so you can monitor where you are at.

TIPS & TRICKS

If you choose to walk trails, remember that all trails are not identified on the map. Use your compass to ensure the trail you are walking runs the same direction as the one on your map.

**Waterproof your map by putting it in a ziplock bag.**

**Keep your scorecard in a ziplock bag as well.**

Take your time conducting your route selection, taking into consideration the total distance you have to walk and the terrain you will have to traverse.

**DO NOT talk to other students on the course.**
**DO NOT lay down to take a nap.**
**DO NOT walk with a flashlight on.**

**When navigating at night, trust your pace count.**

**Remember, at night, 1 click of the bezle ring equals 3 degrees on a lensatic compass!**

Use an M2 Artillery compass to verify the accuracy of your compass. If it is more than 2 degrees off, use a different compass.

The NavStar illuminated compasses only work in the Northern Hemisphere. Remember this if you choose to buy one.

Double safety the compass lanyard. Put it through two loops in case one breaks it is still tied down.

TIPS & TRICKS

Prior to going to SFAS or Delta Selection, ensure you practice land nav with a rucksack on. **This also effects your pace count.**

Often times the shortest route isn't the best route. If your route takes you through a swamp or thick draw, it is better to detour around it even though it is farther.

A wristwatch compass is good to have on your watch for general direction.

**Remember that distance = rate x time**

Know your land nav speed and use it to estimate how long it is going to take you to get to your next point or checkpoint. If you don't know it estimate 2 km/hr. It sounds slow, but it is realistic when you account for map checks, slowdowns, and confusion.

Don't get injured. Be careful, bypass obstacles, wear well broken in boots so you don't blister and maintain your feet.

After several hundred meters, hold your compass in the other hand. Alternating which hand you hold your compass with can help offset drift.

Your pace count is different when travelling uphill versus travelling downhill.

TIPS & TRICKS

## CDMVTAE

**Can Dead Men Vote Twice At Elections**

Compass Deviation Magnetic Variation True Add East

**The Steps:**

Compass - Look at your compass and get your actual reading

Deviation - With a handheld compass this is just limited to compass error

Magnetic - This is your compass reading corrected for deviation

Variation - This is the same as declination from your map sheet

True - This is your bearing, corrected to reference true north

In action it would look like this:

In my area the declination is 10.5 degrees East, and my compass has an error of .5 degrees west. So if I take a compass reading of 232 degrees, the correction to true will look like this:

C - 232
D - subtract .5
M - 231.5
V - add 10.5
T - 242 degrees

To go from True to Magnetic just reverse the process:

## TVMDCAW
True Virgins Make Dull Companions At Weddings

True Variation Magnetic Deviation Compass Add West

Another technique to combat drift is if you are right handed and holding the compass in your right hand, every 100 meters you pace walk 10 meters to the left.

Do Land Nav like you would give somebody directions. "From here head East until you hit a big draw. Bang a left and keep the stream on your right. My house is on the left, if you hit the black top road, you've gone too far."

Never navigate by dead reckoning for more than 500 meters or else you will screw it up.

If you get lost and can find an intersection, stand in the middle of the intersection and shoot an azimuth down every road. Draw a sketch and compare it to your vicinity on the map. Paying attention to the correct angles.

Get good at "compass quickdraw." There are different ways to do it, but make sure your compass is accessible and that you practice drawing/replacing it quickly to encourage frequent checks.

TIPS & TRICKS

If you get momentarily confused between degrees and mils, shoot an azimuth toward the south and if it says "32" then you are looking at 3200 mils, not 32 degrees. Instead look for the number closer to 180.

**Keep your map oriented in the direction you are walking, not North.**

Ensure all of the plastic is trimmed away on your protractor's 1:50,000 scale triangle. Some protractors have too much plastic between where the two 0's meet and this could cause your plots to be off. Use a scalpel or sharp knife to trim it away.

**Grid Lines - Remember Right, Then Up**

# Units of Measure and Conversion Factors

## Equivalent units of angular measure

| | | | |
|---|---|---|---|
| 1 mil | = 1/6400 circle | = 0.05625° | = 0.0625 grad |
| 1 grad | = 1/400 circle | = 16.0 mils | = 0°54' = 0.9° |
| 1 degree | = 1/360 circle | = about 17.8 mils | = about 1.1 grad |

## Ground distance at Map Scale

| SCALE | 1 INCH EQUALS | 1 CENTIMETER EQUALS |
|---|---|---|
| 1:5,000 | 416.67 feet<br>127.00 meters | 164.00 feet<br>50.00 meters |
| 1:10,000 | 833.33 feet<br>254.00 meters | 328.10 feet<br>100.00 meters |
| 1:12,500 | 1,041.66 feet<br>317.00 meters | 410.10 feet<br>125.00 meters |
| 1:20,000 | 1,666.70 feet<br>508.00 meters | 656.20 feet<br>200.00 meters |
| 1:25,000 | 2,083.30 feet<br>635.00 meters | 820.20 feet<br>250.00 meters |
| 1:50,000 | 4,166.70 feet<br>1,270.00 meters | 1,640.40 feet<br>500.00 meters |
| 1:63,360 | 5,280.00 feet<br>1,609.30 meters | 2,078.70 feet<br>633.60 meters |
| 1:100,000 | 8,333.30 feet<br>2,540.00 meters | 3,280.80 feet<br>1,000.00 meters |
| 1:250,000 | 20,833.00 feet<br>6,350.00 meters | 8,202.00 feet<br>2,500.00 meters |
| 1:500,000 | 41,667.00 feet<br>12,700.00 meters | 16,404.00 feet<br>5,000.00 meters |

TIPS & TRICKS

## LINEAR MEASUREMENTS - ENGLISH

| | | |
|---|---|---|
| 12 inches | = | 1 foot |
| 36 inches | = | 1 yard |
| 3 feet | = | 1 yard |
| 1,760 yards | = | 1 mile statute |
| 2,026.8 yards | = | 1 mile nautical |
| 5,280 feet | = | 1 mile statute |
| 6,080.4 feet | = | 1 mile nautical |
| 63,360 inches | = | 1 mile statute |
| 72,963 inches | = | 1 mile nautical |

## LINEAR MEASUREMENTS - METRIC

| | | | | |
|---|---|---|---|---|
| 1 millimeter | = | centimeter | = | 0.0393 inches |
| 10 millimeters | = | centimeter | = | 0.3937 inches |
| 10 centimeters | = | decimeter | = | 3.937 inches |
| 10 decimeters | = | meter | = | 39.37 inches |
| 10 meters | = | decameter | = | 32.81 feet |
| 10 decameters | = | hectometer | = | 328.1 feet |
| 10 hectometers | = | kilometer | = | 0.62 mile |
| 10 kilometers | = | 1.0 myriameter | = | 6.21 miles |

## CONVERSION FACTORS

| ONE | INCHES | FEET | YARDS | STATUTE MILES | NAUTICLE MILES | mm |
|---|---|---|---|---|---|---|
| Inch | 1 | 0.0833 | 0.0277 | - | - | 25.40 |
| Foot | 12 | 1 | 0.333 | - | - | 304.8 |
| Yard | 36 | 3 | 1 | 0.00056 | - | 914.4 |
| Statute Mile | 63,360 | 5,280 | 1,760 | 1 | 0.8684 | - |
| Nautical Mile | 72,963 | 6,080 | 2,026 | 1.1516 | 1 | - |
| Millimeter | 0.0394 | 0.0033 | 0.0011 | - | - | 1 |
| Centimeter | 0.3937 | 0.0328 | 0.0109 | - | - | 10 |
| Decimeter | 3.937 | 0.328 | 0.1093 | - | - | 100 |
| Meter | 39.37 | 3.2808 | 1.0936 | 0.0006 | 0.0005 | 1,000 |
| Decameter | 393.7 | 32.81 | 10.94 | 0.0062 | 0.0054 | 10,000 |
| Hectometer | 3,937 | 328.1 | 109.4 | 0.0621 | 0.0539 | 100,000 |
| Kilometer | 39,370 | 3,281 | 1,094 | 0.6214 | 0.5396 | 1,000,000 |
| Myriameter | 393,700 | 32,808 | 10,936 | 6.2137 | 5.3959 | 10,000,000 |

| ONE | cm | dm | M | dkm | hm | km | mym |
|---|---|---|---|---|---|---|---|
| Inch | 2.540 | 0.2540 | 0.0254 | 0.0025 | 0.0003 | - | - |
| Foot | 30.48 | 3.048 | 0.3048 | 0.0305 | 0.0030 | 0.0003 | - |
| Yard | 91.44 | 9.144 | 0.9144 | 0.0914 | 0.0091 | 0.0009 | - |
| Statute Mile | 160,930 | 16,093 | 1,609 | 160.9 | 16.09 | 1.6093 | 0.1609 |
| Nautical Mile | 185,325 | 18,532 | 1,853 | 185.3 | 18.53 | 1.8532 | 0.1853 |
| Millimeter | 0.1 | 0.01 | 0.001 | 0.0001 | - | - | - |
| Centimeter | 1 | 0.1 | 0.01 | 0.001 | 0.0001 | - | - |
| Decimeter | 10 | 1 | 0.1 | 0.01 | 0.001 | 0.0001 | - |
| Meter | 100 | 1 | 1 | 0.1 | 0.01 | 0.001 | 0.0001 |
| Decameter | 1,000 | 10 | 10 | 1 | 0.1 | 0.01 | 0.001 |
| Hectometer | 10,000 | 100 | 100 | 10 | 1 | 0.1 | 0.01 |
| Kilometer | 100,000 | 1,000 | 1,000 | 100 | 10 | 1 | 0.1 |
| Myriameter | 1,000,000 | 10,000 | 10,000 | 1000 | 100 | 10 | 1 |

TIPS & TRICKS

## NOTES:

# CHAPTER 11:
# RANGER/SF SCHOOL

## RANGER SCHOOL

The Land Nav course at Ranger School is very easy. Don't be overconfident, but I'm going to tell you how easy it is. All of the points are emplaced by Ranger Instructors on 4 wheelers so they are all on trails or right off a trail. Also, the Ranger School Land Nav course is self- correcting. This means that each point has the 8 digit grid to that point on the point itself. My recommendation is to walk the trails (most are on your map) and when you get to a point, look at the grid on that point and plot it to track your progress and see where you are. The trails are lined with points.

The challenge is that you start the course at night. You will need to find 2-3 points at night to have time to finish the course after the sun comes up. Your best bet is to dead reckon to your first point until you hit a dirt trail then walk the trails. If you get to a point and one or more students are at the point, move 10 meters away from the nearest student and take a knee and don't talk to them.

Do NOT get caught walking on the railroad tracks. You can walk the dirt trails, and so will the RI's, but stay off paved roads and the railroad tracks. Do not use your white light while on the course.

Double check all of your plots before starting the course. You don't want to make a mistake before stepping off.

If you find all of your points on the land nav course you get a Major Plus spot report. If you are tight on time and have the 5 of 6 points return to the end point and don't risk running out of time going for the final point.

All Ranger students wear the Cubic GPS trackers. This allows the RI's to be able to find lost Rangers once time is up and they can see if a student is in one place for too long without moving (sleeping). Make sure you hydrate well before starting the course and drink water throughout the course. You do not have to wear a rucksack on the Ranger School land nav course.

Remember all points are emplaced with 4 wheelers so if you are beating brush looking for a point you are probably in the wrong spot. Also, the course is so well travelled, there are many student trails leading right to the points.

You will NOT be taught land navigation at Ranger School. You are expected to already be proficient at land nav so you will only be tested on it. If you fail the land nav course you will be allowed one retest.

### SFAS

You cannot get selected for Special Forces if you cannot pass land navigation. The best land navigation instruction in the Army is at SFAS. You will receive excellent instruction and the cadre will do their very best to help you and teach you. SFAS is changed up fairly regularly, but generally you will do a week of land nav practice tests. These will be day and night and are designed more to put miles on your feet and under your ruck. During the week of practice tests, all points are trucks at intersections. You can parallel, but not handrail your way to every point. For officers all the practice tests count so do your best to find every point at day and night.

The cadre will do a terrain association walk with you in small groups. Take advantage of this time to learn where the main terrain features, crossing points, and intersections are on the test course.

Basically, you will travel using estimated distances, cardinal directions, bouncing between intersections of roads, draws, clearings, etc. Be smart! You will not want or be able to beeline from point to point. You have to do what works for you, not necessarily what works for other people. The terrain walks and practical exercises will help you figure out what approach you want to take.

Make sure you have several checkpoints per klick (1000m) to make sure you are on track. Use backstops so you know if you've overshot your point. Use corridors and handrails like backstops only to the sides. Don't get too close to the roads and violate the rules and make sure you cross all roads at 90 degree angles. The cadre will be out with night vision watching.

## DRAWS

The STAR course is all about those overgrown draws. Even in the winter time they are formidable. Don't bust the draws if you can avoid it, especially at night. Close contour lines mean steep ground which means less water pooling which means less vegetation which means a better place to bust a draw. Find places where other candidates have gone through the draws. They exist, you just have to be patient enough to find them. Worst case you can go all the way around a draw, but you probably can spot a good crossing before that. Check your compass frequently when going through a draw. Check it every 20 steps. It is possible to fight for an hour to end up where you started.

Use attack points! The point sitters have to get dropped off at intersections by trucks and then walk a little ways into the woods. You should be able to identify an attack point on the map to navigate to and then dead reckon from your attack point to your point. A good attack point is 300 meters or less from your point. Use SLLS (Stop, Look, Listen, Smell) when you get near your point. Some of the point sitters are crafty!

## OWN THE NIGHT

A majority of your time will be during the dark hours. You cannot wait for the sun to rise and then get busy. Many of the points are easier to find at night because they will have a chemlight or campfire.

Make up time when you are on nonrestrictive terrain. You will lose time at the crossings, searching for points, and busting draws. Do NOT forget to think. Land Nav is a thinking man's game. Don't be too focused on moving quickly that you make mistakes. Make sure you judiciously mark your map. Don't overmark or you'll cover good information. Don't undermark because you'll be surprised how well you remember a specific moment from before if you take the right notes.

On the STAR course, also known as the Hoffman course, you will need to find all 4 of your points on the first day or 9 points over 3 days in order to pass. You will only be given one point at a time. Once you reach that point you will be given your next point. If I remember correctly, the points are around 10 km apart. The STAR course got its name from the shape you get when you connect your points. Make sure you tie your map and compass down. Don't talk to other candidates. Don't lay down to take a nap. If you make a stupid mistake, stay with it and don't give in. Don't get caught dumping water from your 2 quart canteens on your rucksack to lighten your load.

Prior to test day, you should know where all of the below are located:

- The TOC
- 3-Wire Road
- 4-Wire Road
- Puppy Palace
- Bowling Alley
- Six Points
- Jurassic Park-Big draw to the west
- Lookout Tower (North of Jurassic Park)
- Five Points (South of Jurassic Park)
- Lake Baggett and its authorized crossing
- SCUBA Road and its dry crossing
- Dagobah

Note any stakes during practice that are engineer stakes with a dogtag and a grid coordinate on them.

# More by Bronston Clough...

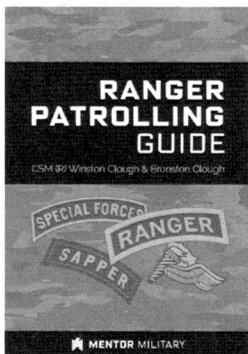

## Ranger Patrolling Guide

Master the art of patrolling, and learn the skills of the light, fast, and lethal Ranger patrol. Contains tips, tricks, and lessons learned from the field.

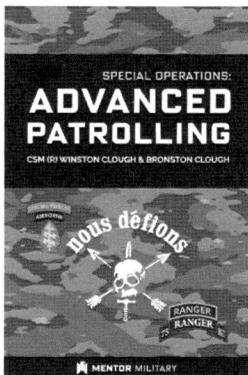

## Specials Operations: Advanced Patrolling

The book also contains tips and tricks for foot care, packing your rucksack, and advanced weapons maintenance. Every Soldier from Infantry to Special Operations can learn from this book.

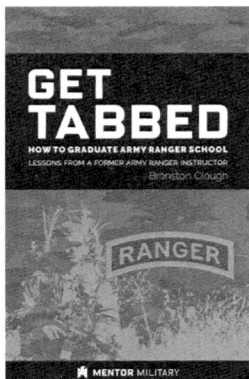

## Get Tabbed

Learn how to graduate Army Ranger School with the tips and lessons from a former Army Ranger Instructor.

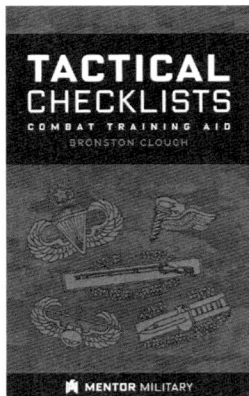

## Tactical Checklists

An effective unit is a well-trained unit. Leave nothing to chance. Keep yourself and your Soldiers prepared with this book of tactical checklists.

Find these titles and much more at **MentorMilitary.com**